CONSULTING HANDBOOK

JACK PRZEMIENIECKI

ISBN: 9798866762972

First published November 2023

www.hownottofailatconsulting.com

To Magdalena.

Contents

Introduction

Starting a career in consulting is like getting on a rollercoaster. You're excited, nervous, and maybe a little bit queasy all at the same time. You'll spend hours pouring over data, creating presentations, and trying to understand issues you barely knew existed. Just when you think you've got it all figured out, your boss will throw you for a loop and say, "Great job, but we need to pivot and go in a completely different direction." Don't worry; the ups and downs are all part of consulting. One day, you'll feel like you're on top of the world; the next, you'll be reeling under a mountain of data and deadlines. So, hold on tight!

Consulting is all about helping organisations solve complex problems, make better decisions, and achieve their objectives. It's a dynamic and fast-paced industry that requires a combination of technical expertise, problem-solving, and critical thinking skills. You'll need to be adaptable, flexible, and able to thrive in an ever-changing environment. Ultimately, consulting is a challenging and rewarding career that requires consistency, perseverance, and determination.

However, being a consultant goes beyond only solving problems. You'll work with diverse clients, stakeholders, and colleagues, each with unique personalities, goals, and expectations. As such, you'll need to develop top-notch communication and interpersonal skills, including active listening, empathy, and conflict resolution. You must go beyond being a walking encyclopedia of business jargon and instead aspire to become a well-rounded, open-minded, and humble leader with an unwavering commitment to continuous learning and self-improvement.

With this handbook as your trusty guide, you'll be well on your way to conquering the consulting world in no time. So grab a cup of coffee (or six), take a deep breath, and get ready to dive headfirst into the consulting world. It's going to be a wild ride. Still, with a little bit of humour and a whole lot of determination, you'll be delivering high-quality work and exceeding your client's expectations in no time. Let's do this!

"The people who are crazy enough
to think they can change the world
are the ones who do."

Steve Jobs

1.0 Basics

Consultants, those elusive beings that float around office spaces with their laptops, can be a bit of a mystery. What exactly do they do all day? Are they even doing anything? Why do they insist on throwing the words "synergy", "leverage", and "disruptive innovation" into every conversation?

Despite the seemingly endless sea of jargon and the occasional existential crisis induced by a 100-slide presentation deck, there's something alluring about the consulting world. It's a place where problems are tackled head-on, solutions are devised and implemented, and every day is a chance to learn something new. If you have already landed a position at a consulting firm, you may proceed directly to Chapter 3. Otherwise, continue reading to embark on your consulting journey.

Definition

Consulting is a professional service that provides expert advice and guidance to individuals, businesses, governments, and organisations in a particular field or area of expertise.

Services

Consulting services encompass various areas, including management, IT, finance, HR, marketing, sustainability, healthcare, and legal. They provide strategic advice and solutions to individuals and organisations, assisting with business operations, technology, finance, human resources, marketing, industry-specific challenges, and more. Consultants offer tailored insights and recommendations to drive success and competitiveness in their respective fields.

Clients

Consulting clients can come from various industries, sectors, and backgrounds. Some consulting clients are large multinational corporations that require specialised expertise and guidance to navigate complex business challenges. Other clients may be small or medium-sized businesses that need help with specific issues such as financial management or marketing strategy. Non-profit organisations and government agencies may also seek out consulting services to help them achieve their mission and goals. The range of consulting clients is vast, and consultants tailor their services to meet each client's needs.

Benefits

Joining the consulting industry can offer many benefits, such as exposure to different industries and clients, challenging projects, professional development opportunities, financial rewards, career advancement opportunities, a strong network of professional contacts, and flexibility and variety. However, there are also challenges, such as long hours, travel requirements, lack of control over project assignments, high expectations and pressure to perform, limited job security, and a lack of work-life balance.

The consulting industry is a diverse and dynamic field that provides a range of services to businesses and organisations across various industries. Consulting firms work closely with clients to provide tailored solutions to complex problems, drawing on the skills and expertise of their consultants.

While there are potential drawbacks to joining the consulting industry, consulting can offer an exciting and fulfilling career path for those with a strong interest in problem-solving, intellectual curiosity, and a desire to make a significant impact.

1.1 Grades

Going up the grades in consulting is like evolutions in a game of Pokémon. You start as a lowly associate and work up the ladder, evolving into more complex and powerful forms. First, you're an associate, then a consultant, then a manager, a director, and finally, a partner. It's like levelling up; except instead of fighting battles, you're battling Excel spreadsheets and PowerPoint presentations. Each level has challenges, from learning new skills to dealing with demanding clients. You'll face more prominent clients and complex projects that will test your skills and push you to your limits. So, grab your Poké Ball (or laptop) and get ready to level up!

Associate
Entry-level associate consultants are responsible for conducting research, data analysis, and assisting in project tasks. They support senior consultants in gathering information, creating reports, and developing recommendations.

Consultant
Consultants take on more responsibilities, such as managing project components, conducting interviews, and analysing data. They collaborate with clients and teams to develop strategies, solve problems, and produce project deliverables.

Manager
These professionals provide leadership and guidance to junior team members. They oversee project execution, client interactions, and quality control. Managers are responsible for developing and maintaining client relationships and may specialise in specific industries or domains.

Director

Directors are responsible for managing large-scale projects, overseeing multiple teams, and building strong client relationships. They provide strategic guidance, drive business development efforts, and play a crucial role in shaping the direction and growth of the consulting practice.

Partner

Partners are senior leaders within consulting firms. They are responsible for the overall direction and management of the firm. They drive business development, build and maintain client relationships, and oversee the delivery of projects. They provide high-level strategic advice, mentor junior consultants, and contribute to the firm's thought leadership.

The consulting industry offers a clear path to career progression but requires hard work, dedication, and a commitment to ongoing learning and development. By focusing on building skills, gaining experience, and demonstrating leadership, consultants can advance through the ranks and achieve success in this challenging and rewarding field.

1.2 Benefits

The glamorous life of a consultant: endless hours of data crunching, PowerPoint presentations, and pretending to understand industry jargon. But let's remember the perks of the job! You get to travel to exotic locations, stay in budget hotels with questionable cleanliness standards, and eat meals that are 50% per diem and 50% regret. Plus, you get to impress your friends and family with your ability to recite random statistics and business buzzwords that nobody else understands. It can be an arduous journey, but at least you'll never be bored.

Exposure

As a consultant, you will work with various businesses and industries, giving you a unique perspective and broad exposure to different types of companies. This exposure will enable you to develop a deep understanding of various industries and business models.

New challenges

Consulting projects are typically complex and challenging, requiring high intellectual curiosity and creative problem-solving skills. You will be tasked with developing innovative solutions to help businesses achieve their goals. These projects will give you a sense of fulfilment and enable you to impact your clients' organisations significantly.

Professional development

Consulting firms invest heavily in the professional development of their employees. You will receive extensive training, mentorship, and coaching to help you develop your skills and advance your career. These opportunities can help you build a strong career foundation and accelerate your professional growth.

Financial rewards

Consulting firms offer competitive salaries, bonuses, and benefits packages. These rewards can be particularly attractive for those early in their careers or looking to transition from other industries. As you gain experience and build your skills, you can take on more senior roles within the firm, leading to even higher compensation levels.

Advancement opportunities

The consulting industry offers many opportunities for career advancement. As you gain experience and develop your skills, you can advance within the firm, taking on additional responsibilities such as managing projects or leading teams. Additionally, consulting experience can be valuable for those looking to transition to other roles within the business world.

Strong network

As a consultant, you will work with clients from different industries, enabling you to build a strong network of professional contacts. These connections can be valuable for future career opportunities and may lead to new business opportunities for your consulting firm.

Flexibility and variety

Consulting offers flexibility in terms of project types, industries, and locations. This flexibility can attract those who value variety and want to work on projects that align with their interests and strengths.

The consulting industry offers many benefits. From exposure to various industries and clients to challenging and complex projects, professional development opportunities, financial rewards, career advancement opportunities, a strong network of professional contacts, and flexibility and variety, consulting can provide a fulfilling and rewarding career path. If you are looking for an exciting and dynamic career that allows you to make a significant impact, then joining the consulting industry may be the right choice for you.

1.3 Negatives

Let's be honest; consulting isn't all sunshine and rainbows. You'll spend countless hours staring at spreadsheets, trying to decipher data that makes no sense, and sitting through meetings that feel like they'll never end. Then there's the incessant stream of emails and phone calls that come in at all hours of the day and night, reminding you that you're never really off the clock. Plus, you'll have to deal with difficult clients who make unreasonable demands and coworkers who are more concerned with impressing the boss than actually getting work done. Acknowledging these hurdles, seeking guidance, and finding a healthy work-life balance are crucial steps to preparing yourself for the realities of the consulting industry.

Long hours
Consulting can blur the boundaries between work and personal life. The workload can be challenging to manage and may lead to burnout if not adequately addressed. You'll need to prioritise effective time management, set expectations with clients and team members, delegate tasks when possible, and establish boundaries to maintain a healthy work-life balance.

Travel requirements
Depending on the consulting firm and the nature of the project, travel may be a significant part of the job. Extended periods of being away from home may impact personal relationships, particularly for consultants with family or other obligations. You'll have to practice self-care, optimise travel arrangements, and manage expectations with loved ones.

Lack of control
As a consultant, you may not have control over which projects you work on and working on projects that do not align with your interests or career goals can be frustrating and demotivating. You'll need to manage your career by actively networking within your firm, identifying your areas of interest, and proactively working towards your objectives.

High pressure

Consulting projects can involve demanding clients and managers who expect exceptional results. To mitigate this challenge, clearly set project scope and deliverables, maintain transparent communication, manage client expectations effectively, and focus on building strong relationships based on trust and collaboration.

Office politics

As with many industries, the consulting industry can be highly competitive regarding promotions and advancement. This competition can be intense, and not everyone may be able to achieve their desired career trajectory within their firm. Internal competition and office politics can be challenging to navigate. You'll need to focus on collaboration rather than competition, build strong relationships with colleagues based on mutual respect and support, maintain professionalism in all interactions, and strive for open and transparent communication.

A career in consulting comes with its fair share of challenges, including long hours, travel requirements, lack of control over projects, high-pressure environments, and office politics. However, by acknowledging these hurdles and implementing effective mitigation strategies, such as prioritising work-life balance, practising self-care, seeking guidance, managing expectations, and fostering positive relationships, you can navigate the realities of the consulting industry and thrive in your career. Remember that resilience, adaptability, and a proactive approach to personal and professional growth are vital to succeeding in the consulting world.

1.4 Preparation

Preparing for a career in consulting is like training for a marathon, except instead of running, you're doing mental gymnastics. You'll spend hours reading business books, watching TED talks, and practising your presentation skills. You'll learn how to sound confident even when you have no idea what you're talking about and how to navigate the treacherous waters of office politics. But don't worry; all that preparation will pay off when you finally land that consulting job and can impress your colleagues with your ability to create beautiful graphs on the fly.

Education and experience
A solid academic background in business, finance, economics, or a related field is typically required for a career in consulting. Additionally, gaining experience through internships or part-time work in relevant industries can be beneficial.

Develop relevant skills
Consulting firms value strong analytical skills, problem-solving abilities, communication skills, project management capabilities, and attention to detail. Developing these skills through coursework, extracurricular activities, or other experiences can be valuable.

Research the industry
Gain a thorough understanding of the consulting industry, the types of consulting firms, and the services they provide. Research firms of interest to learn about their culture, values, and client base.

Build a network
Attend career fairs, industry events, and other networking opportunities to meet people and learn about potential job opportunities. Don't be shy about contacting people on LinkedIn. Of course, some may not respond, but others may be open to providing advice, guidance, or mentorship.

Develop a strong resume

Tailor your resume and cover letter to the consulting industry, highlighting your relevant experience, skills, and education. Be sure to emphasise your problem-solving and analytical skills. Use a modern, clean template, and review your resume for consistency, spelling and grammar.

Apply to consulting firms

Once you have developed your skills and gained relevant experience, apply to consulting firms of interest. Be prepared for a rigorous interview process, including multiple rounds of interviews, case studies, and behavioural assessments.

Preparing for a career in the consulting industry requires a combination of education, experience, skills, research, networking, and perseverance. By focusing on these areas and developing a comprehensive understanding of the industry, you can position yourself for success in a rewarding and challenging career.

"You miss 100% of the shots you don't take."

Wayne Gretzky

2.0 Interviews

Preparing for interviews can be a nerve-wracking experience, but it's essential if you want to land that dream consulting job. You will spend weeks researching the company, practising case studies, and memorising business buzzwords. You'll practice your handshake until it's firm but not too firm and your smile until it's friendly but not too friendly. All that preparation will pay off when you finally walk into that interview room and dazzle the interviewers with your perfectly crafted answers and flawless eye contact. Just remember to breathe, smile, and avoid any mention of your obsession with cat videos on YouTube.

Research the firm
Before the interview, research the firm thoroughly to understand the firm's history, values, services, and clients. Look for recent news articles, social media posts, and other information to understand the organisation comprehensively.

Understand the format

Consulting firms often use a structured interview format, which may include multiple rounds of interviews, case studies, and behavioural assessments. Understanding the format will help you prepare for each stage of the interview process.

Prepare examples

Consulting firms often use behavioural questions to evaluate candidates' past experiences and how they approach problems. Prepare examples of past experiences demonstrating your problem-solving abilities, teamwork skills, and leadership capabilities.

Practice case studies

Case studies are a common part of the consulting interview process, and they evaluate candidates' problem-solving abilities and analytical skills. Develop your case study skills by researching sample case studies online and practice solving them with a mentor.

Highlight your experience

During the interview, emphasise your relevant skills and experience, such as your analytical skills, project management capabilities, and attention to detail. Use specific examples to demonstrate your abilities and keep your answers structured.

Show enthusiasm

Consulting firms look for candidates who are enthusiastic about the industry and demonstrate a curiosity for problem-solving. Show your enthusiasm by asking thoughtful questions and expressing interest in the firm and its clients.

Dress professionally

The consulting industry values professionalism and punctuality. Dress professionally, and arrive early to demonstrate your reliability.

Follow up

After the interview, send a thank-you note to the interviewer or interviewers, as it can help you stand out and demonstrate your interest in the position.

Preparing for an interview in the consulting industry requires research, practice, preparation, and professionalism. By understanding the format, practising case studies, preparing examples of past experiences, highlighting your relevant skills, showing enthusiasm, dressing professionally, and following up after the interview, you can position yourself for success.

2.1 Interview types

Consulting interviews are like playing an adventure video game, except all the endings lead to PowerPoint presentations. There's the standard behavioural interview, where you have to explain how you dealt with a problematic coworker without bursting into tears. Then there's the case interview, where you're given a hypothetical problem that may have nothing to do with your actual job and asked to solve it on the spot while the interviewer looks at you like you're a contestant on a reality TV show. Finally, let's not forget about the group interview, where you're thrown into a room with strangers and asked to collaborate on a project while secretly plotting to sabotage them all and emerge victorious.

Behavioural interviews

Designed to assess a candidate's past experiences and how they approach problem-solving. Questions may include "Tell me about a time when you had to solve a complex problem" or "Describe a situation where you had to work in a team to achieve a goal." Candidates should prepare examples of past experiences demonstrating their problem-solving, teamwork, and leadership capabilities.

Case interviews

Typical in the consulting industry and are used to evaluate a candidate's problem-solving abilities and analytical skills. Candidates are presented with a business problem and asked to develop a solution. The interviewer is interested in how the candidate approaches the problem, the logic behind their solution, and their ability to communicate their thought process.

Technical interviews

They are designed to evaluate a candidate's technical skills and knowledge in a specific area. For example, candidates may be asked to demonstrate their understanding of financial analysis, marketing strategy, or supply chain management.

Group interviews

They are usually employed to assess a candidate's teamwork skills and ability to collaborate with others. Candidates may be asked to work on a group project or solve a problem as a team. The interviewer is interested in how the candidate interacts with others, how they communicate their ideas, and their ability to compromise.

Final round interviews

Typically, the last stage of the interview process involves meeting with senior leaders at the firm. The focus may be on assessing the candidate's fit with the firm's culture, values, and leadership potential.

The consulting industry uses various interview types to evaluate candidates' skills, knowledge, and fit with the firm's culture. By understanding the different types of interviews, candidates can better prepare for the interview process and improve their chances of not making a complete mess of it. That said, even if an interview does not go well, don't be too hard on yourself. Use it as a learning experience, ask the interviewer for detailed feedback to identify areas of improvement, and do better on the next one.

2.2 Outfits

First impressions matter, and what you wear to a professional interview can significantly impact how the interviewer perceives you. On the one hand, you want to look professional and polished, but on the other hand, you don't want to look like you just walked off the set of The Wolf of Wall Street. It's like Goldilocks trying to find the perfect porridge: not too hot or cold, but just right. You'll spend hours trying on different suits and ties, experimenting with different hairstyles, or debating whether to wear heels or flats. It's a delicate balance, but with some luck and a good tailor, you might just nail that perfect interview outfit. Remember to avoid anything too flashy, tight, or reminiscent of your high school prom.

Choose a conservative outfit

When in doubt, it's always better to err on the side of caution and choose a more conservative outfit. You can never be overdressed, but you can undoubtedly be underdressed. A dark-coloured suit, dress pants or skirt, and a collared shirt or blouse are all appropriate options for a professional interview. Avoid wearing bright or flashy colours, patterns, or accessories that can be distracting.

Pay attention to fit

Make sure that your outfit fits well and is comfortable to wear. Clothes that are too tight or too loose can be distracting and uncomfortable. Try on your outfit ahead of time to ensure that it looks professional and that you feel comfortable wearing it.

Keep accessories to a minimum

While accessories can add some personality to your outfit, keeping them to a minimum is essential. Avoid wearing anything that could be considered too ostentatious or distracting. Remember, the focus should be on your skills and qualifications, not your accessories.

Dress appropriately for the job

While a conservative outfit is generally a safe choice for a professional interview, it's also important to dress appropriately for the job you are applying for. If you are applying for a creative position, you may be able to get away with a more casual outfit. However, if you are applying for a more formal role, it's best to stick with a conservative option. Ask the hiring manager or someone in a similar position for advice when in doubt.

Dressing appropriately for a professional interview shows that you are serious about the opportunity and have put in the effort to make a good impression. By researching the company culture, choosing a conservative outfit that fits well, and keeping accessories to a minimum, you can ensure that you make a great first impression on your interviewer.

2.3 Introductory interview

Introductory interviews are like speed dating, but with less romance and more anxiety. You have just a few minutes to make an excellent first impression, dazzle the interviewer with your sparkling personality, and convince them that you're the perfect candidate for the job. It's like trying to cram your entire life story into a tiny soundbite while avoiding mentioning your awkward middle school phase. You'll practise your elevator pitch until it's as smooth as butter, and you'll come up with clever responses to common questions like "Tell me about yourself." Remember to smile, be yourself, and don't ramble on about your preoccupation with collectable figurines.

Research the company

Before the interview, thoroughly research the company's history, mission, values, and culture. This knowledge will help you prepare for the interview questions and demonstrate your genuine interest in the company. For example, research the company's clients, projects, and recent press releases.

Prepare responses

The hiring manager can ask about your qualifications, work experience, and personal background. Be sure to have concise and well-thought-out responses prepared for these questions. For instance, if asked to describe your strengths, provide examples of how you used your strengths in previous projects or work experiences.

Structure your responses

The STAR approach helps structure responses in an interview. When asked a behavioural question, describe the Situation or context of the challenge you faced. Then, explain the Task or goal you were trying to achieve. Next, define the Action you took to solve the problem using specific examples and details. Finally, share the Result or outcome of your actions and how they positively impacted the situation.

Highlight your accomplishments

During the interview, highlight your achievements, showcasing your technical abilities. Be specific and provide evidence of your successes. For example, if describing a previous marketing role, share how you increased website traffic or social media engagement.

Ask questions

At the end of the interview, the interviewer will typically ask if you have any questions. Use this opportunity to ask insightful and relevant questions about the company and the position, demonstrating your interest and eagerness to learn more about the company. For example, you can ask about the company's culture, training programs, or work environment.

Follow up

After the interview, send a thank-you email to the interviewer to express your appreciation for the opportunity and to reiterate your interest in the job. For instance, you can mention a particular aspect of the company or the position that excites you.

Succeeding in an introductory competency interview requires thorough preparation, effective communication, and a positive attitude. By researching the company, preparing responses to common questions, highlighting your accomplishments, demonstrating your skills, showing your passion, asking questions, and following up, you can leave a lasting impression on the interviewer and enhance your prospects of advancing to subsequent interview stages.

2.4 Case study interview

Case study interviews are like being dropped into a foreign country without a map or a phrasebook. You'll be given a complex business problem to solve, and you'll need to come up with a brilliant solution on the spot, all while pretending like you know what you're doing. You'll scribble furiously on a piece of paper, trying to remember all the business jargon you memorised, and you'll nod vigorously to convince the interviewer that you're making sense. Remember to take deep breaths, keep calm, and resist the urge to throw the paper across the room and run screaming out of the building.

Understand the case

Before the interview, review the case study materials, if any are provided. Understand the context, problem statement, and objectives of the case study. Take note of any assumptions or constraints given.

Analyse the case

Analyse the case study materials and identify the key issues and factors that should be considered. Use frameworks and tools to structure your analysis, and be sure to explain your approach and reasoning.

Organise your thoughts

Structure your responses to the questions asked by the interviewer. Be clear and concise, and use data and evidence to support your arguments. For example, if asked to recommend a solution for a business problem, provide a clear and well-supported argument for why that solution is the best course of action.

Collaborate with the interviewer

The case study interview is an opportunity to demonstrate your collaboration skills. Work with the interviewer to understand their perspective and ask clarifying questions. Take their feedback and incorporate it into your analysis.

Manage your time

If there is a time constraint to the case study, plan accordingly, giving yourself enough time for analysis, writing and review. Prioritise the structure to demonstrate your approach and logic rather than spending too much time on superfluous details.

Communicate effectively

The interviewer assesses your communication skills, so articulate your ideas clearly and concisely. If appropriate, use visual aids like graphs and charts to support your analysis, and be prepared to explain them.

Be creative

The interviewer wants to see how you think outside the box. Be creative and innovative in your approach, and don't be afraid to challenge assumptions. For example, if asked to develop a new product idea, think beyond traditional products and consider unique and unconventional ideas.

Practice, practice, practice

Practice with peers or mentors to hone your skills. Use online resources to access sample case studies and simulate the interview environment as closely as possible. Repetitive practice will help you become more comfortable with the interview process and improve your performance.

Succeeding in a case study interview requires thorough preparation, effective communication, and a creative approach. By understanding the case, analysing it, organising your thoughts, collaborating with the interviewer, communicating effectively, being creative, and practising, you can impress the interviewer and increase your chances of landing the job. Remember to be confident, professional, and genuine, and you will be well on your way to success.

2.5 Group interview

Group interviews are like a reality TV show. You'll be thrown into a room with a bunch of strangers, all vying for the same job, and you'll need to work together to solve a complex business problem. You'll try to assert your dominance without coming across as a total jerk, and you'll try to contribute without sounding like a know-it-all. Remember to be a team player, listen to the ideas of others, and refrain from forming covert partnerships with individuals who appear to know what they are doing.

Be collaborative

During the interview, demonstrate your collaboration skills. Listen to others' ideas and opinions, and encourage them to share their thoughts. Build on each other's ideas and work towards a common goal. For example, if you are tasked with a group brainstorming session to devise a solution to a business problem, listen actively to your peers and add value to their suggestions.

Be a leader

The group interview is an opportunity to showcase your leadership potential. Take the initiative and contribute ideas. Offer to be the timekeeper or to structure the group's approach. Be willing to take on tasks and responsibilities and ensure the group stays on track. For example, if the group is tasked with presenting a solution to a business problem, take charge of organising the presentation and ensure that everyone has a role to play.

Communicate effectively

Communicating effectively in a group interview is crucial for making a positive impression and showcasing your abilities. You will impress the interviewer and other participants by actively listening, contributing thoughtfully and engaging respectfully. Avoid dominating the conversation or being dismissive or confrontational.

For example, when discussing a hypothetical scenario, you could actively listen to your peers' ideas, build upon them by suggesting practical solutions, and respectfully seek consensus by encouraging open dialogue. By demonstrating strong communication skills, you can effectively convey your expertise, collaborative nature, and ability to work well within a team.

Embrace diversity

Remain open-minded to different perspectives that emerge from the diverse group. For instance, when discussing a global business problem in a group interview, leverage your peers' cultural and professional expertise to develop a well-rounded solution considering diverse perspectives. By embracing diversity, you can demonstrate your ability to collaborate effectively and think inclusively.

Be confident

Finally, be confident in yourself and your abilities. Be assertive when presenting your ideas; use evidence and data to support your arguments. Also, be willing to accept constructive feedback and use it to improve your performance.

Just like on a reality TV show, avoid being the know-it-all, the aggressor, or the quiet one that says nothing at all. By being collaborative, a leader, communicating effectively, being professional, embracing diversity, and being confident, you can impress the hiring team and increase your chances of landing the job.

"Success is a journey, not a destination."

Arthur Ashe

3.0 Welcome

Congratulations, you have secured a job in consulting! The first few weeks in a new job can be overwhelming and challenging, but with the right approach, you can make a smooth transition and set yourself up for success. You'll be given a crash course on everything from industry jargon to office politics while also trying to remember everyone's name. You'll be inundated with information, trying to keep up with the barrage of emails and meeting requests. Remember to take deep breaths, ask lots of questions, and resist the urge to curl up under your desk and cry. Eventually, you'll get the hang of it, or at least pretend to.

Learn about the company

In the first few weeks of a consulting job, take time to learn about the company, its culture, and its values. Attend orientation sessions, read the company's website and social media pages, and familiarise yourself with the company's mission and vision. This knowledge will help you understand the company's expectations and align your goals with the organisation's.

Develop a network

Networking and building relationships with colleagues are essential in consulting. Take time to introduce yourself, ask questions, and get to know your colleagues. Identify the key stakeholders and understand their roles and responsibilities. Building strong relationships will help you collaborate effectively, gain support, and navigate the company's culture.

Get on a project

The best way to learn about the company and build relationships is to join a project. The tricky part is finding a project aligned with your experience and areas of interest. Reach out to project leaders, find out what they are working on, and don't be afraid to pitch yourself for a role. Remember that if you don't find a project for yourself, there is a high probability that you'll be assigned a project role that no one else wants.

Create a plan

Identify objectives and work towards them. For example, challenge yourself to reach out to a certain number of people you've yet to meet every week. By setting personal objectives and working towards them, you'll avoid distractions and have a clear plan to follow.

Be proactive

Take the initiative to learn and contribute to your project or team. Ask questions and clarify expectations to ensure that you understand the project requirements. Also, be willing to take on additional responsibilities and challenges to demonstrate your willingness to learn and contribute.

Communicate effectively

In consulting, effective communication is paramount. Its significance is emphasised throughout the upcoming chapters, where we delve into various communication-related aspects. In short, prioritise clarity and conciseness, practice active listening, steer clear of jargon, and adapt your communication style to suit your audience.

Manage your time

Time management is crucial in consulting jobs where you may be working on multiple projects simultaneously. Prioritise your tasks, set deadlines, and use tools like calendars and project management software to manage your time effectively. Also, communicate your availability to your colleagues and manager to avoid overcommitting and missing deadlines.

Identify learning opportunities

Consulting offers many opportunities for learning and growth. Seek feedback from your colleagues and manager on your performance and identify areas for improvement. Also, take advantage of training and development programs offered by the company to enhance your skills and knowledge.

Succeeding in the first weeks of a consulting job requires a proactive and positive attitude, effective communication, time management, goal setting, building relationships, seeking feedback, and identifying learning opportunities. By following these tips and leveraging your unique strengths and qualities, you can smoothly transition to your new role and set yourself up for success in your consulting career. Keep an open mind to new challenges and embrace the opportunities to learn and grow that come with working in consulting.

3.1 Core skills

To succeed in a career in consulting, you need to be like a ninja: stealthy, agile, and able to solve complex problems with a single blow (or Excel formula). You'll need to adapt to any situation, whether analysing financial statements or leading a team of confused executives through a brainstorming session. Be the black belt of time management, juggling multiple projects and deadlines without breaking a sweat (or at least without anyone noticing).

Develop your skills

To succeed in consulting, you must continually develop your skills and expertise, acquiring a deep understanding of emerging technologies, market trends, and best practices. Stay current on industry news, attend conferences and workshops, and pursue certifications and advanced degrees to expand your knowledge and expertise.

Build relationships

Engage with clients and colleagues by being a good listener, understanding their needs and concerns, and providing thoughtful and practical solutions to their problems. Always be honest, transparent, and responsive to their feedback and concerns.

Build your brand

Attend industry events, join professional organisations, and connect with consultants and industry experts to build your network and establish yourself as a thought leader. Utilise social media and other digital marketing channels to develop your brand and demonstrate your expertise and credibility.

Develop project management skills

Plan and execute projects efficiently and effectively, manage budgets and resources, and communicate clearly with team members and clients.

Develop your project management skills by taking courses, learning from colleagues, attending workshops, and practising on real-world projects.

Embrace collaboration

Consulting is a team sport; success depends on collaborating with other consultants, team members, and clients. Be willing to listen, share ideas, collaborate on solutions, and always be open to feedback and constructive criticism. Embracing a collaborative approach will help you build strong relationships, deliver better outcomes, and establish yourself as a valuable team member.

Stay agile and adaptable

Adapting to changing circumstances and pivoting as needed is essential in the fast-paced consulting world. Stay agile and flexible, and be willing to adjust your approach and strategies as needed. Be proactive in identifying potential roadblocks and challenges, and work with your team and clients to develop creative solutions and strategies to overcome these obstacles.

Focus on delivering value

Ultimately, success in consulting depends on your ability to deliver value to clients, focusing on their needs and concerns, providing effective solutions that meet their goals and objectives, and continually striving to improve and innovate. Always be results-oriented and focus on delivering measurable outcomes that demonstrate the value of your services and expertise.

Succeeding as a consultant requires a combination of skills, qualities, and strategies that can help you build strong relationships, develop expertise, be adaptable, communicate effectively, and deliver results. By focusing on these areas and continuously improving your skills and knowledge, you can build a successful and rewarding career in consulting.

3.2 Teamwork

Teamwork makes the dream work, or so they say. Working in teams is a critical aspect of consulting, as most consulting projects require a collaborative effort among team members to deliver high-quality results. But let's be honest, sometimes teamwork can feel more like a nightmare, especially when team members have different personalities, objectives, communication styles, and working preferences. It's like playing in a rock band, requiring us to acknowledge each band member for their unique skills, strengths, and perspectives, harmonising to create something far greater than the sum of its parts.

Define roles and responsibilities

One of the essential steps in effective teamwork is to define roles and responsibilities for each team member. In consulting, team members come from diverse backgrounds and have different skill sets, so assigning tasks based on each member's strengths and expertise is crucial. The team leader should clearly communicate the roles and responsibilities to ensure everyone is on the same page. This will minimise confusion and ensure everyone is working towards a common goal. For example, suppose a consulting team is working on a project for a retail company to improve its sales strategy. In that case, the team leader can assign one team member to conduct market research, another to analyse data, and another to develop recommendations based on the research and analysis.

Establish clear communication

Team members must be able to communicate effectively to ensure that everyone is on the same page and that the project is progressing as planned. Establishing clear communication channels and protocols from the outset is critical. For example, the consulting team can set up regular team meetings to discuss progress, share updates, and identify potential roadblocks. They can also use collaborative tools such as shared project management software or communication platforms to facilitate real-time communication.

Foster collaboration and trust

Trust and effective collaboration among team members is essential for achieving project objectives. Fostering a culture that promotes open communication, idea sharing, and challenging assumptions strengthens group unity. For instance, brainstorming sessions encourage the consulting team to generate ideas and share perspectives. Additionally, assigning team members to work together in pairs or groups enhances collaboration and knowledge sharing.

Leverage each other's strengths

Consulting teams are often composed of individuals with diverse skill sets, backgrounds, and expertise. Leveraging each team member's strengths is essential to complete the project successfully. For example, if a project requires the analysis of complex financial data, seek out team members with a finance background to ensure the analysis is accurate and reliable.

Manage conflicts effectively

In any team, conflicts are inevitable, and how they are managed can make or break the team's effectiveness. Conflicts can arise due to differences in opinion, communication breakdowns, or competing priorities. For example, suppose a consulting team is working on a project where there is a disagreement about the best approach to solve a particular problem. The team leader can facilitate a discussion and encourage team members to present their arguments while listening to others' perspectives. The team leader can then guide the team towards a mutually agreed-upon solution.

Effective teamwork is essential in consulting, and the abovementioned strategies can help teams work together effectively. Defining roles and responsibilities, establishing clear communication, fostering collaboration and trust, leveraging each other's strengths, and effectively managing conflicts can all contribute to a successful consulting project. By following these strategies, consulting teams can improve productivity, increase client satisfaction, and achieve project objectives.

3.3 Problem-solving

Effective problem-solving and critical thinking are the superpowers that transform mere mortals into unstoppable superhero consultants, soaring through the corporate skies in their spandex suits. Armed with laser-sharp analysis and a utility belt of brainstorming gadgets, they swoop into boardrooms like caped crusaders, ready to tackle the most perplexing challenges. By employing strong problem-solving abilities, consultants can dissect intricate problems, break them down into manageable components, and apply analytical thinking to devise innovative strategies.

Develop a structured approach

The ability to approach problems in a structured way involves breaking down complex problems into smaller, more manageable components and clearly understanding the underlying issues and root causes. A structured approach ensures that all relevant information is considered and solutions are developed logically and coherently. For example, a consulting team working with a manufacturing company might use a structured approach to address issues with product quality. The approach could involve conducting a root cause analysis to identify the underlying issues, developing a set of hypotheses about potential solutions, and testing those hypotheses through experiments and data analyses.

Ask the right questions

Critical thinking and problem-solving require asking the right questions to understand the problem at hand and the broader context in which the problem exists. Consultants must be able to ask insightful and thought-provoking questions that challenge assumptions, uncover hidden biases, and reveal important insights. For example, a consulting team working with a healthcare provider might ask questions such as "What are the underlying factors driving the high cost of healthcare in this region?" or "How can we better align incentives to encourage more efficient use of healthcare resources?"

Use data to inform decision-making

In today's data-driven world, consultants need to be able to analyse and interpret data to inform their decision-making. A solid grasp of statistical analysis, data visualisation, and the capacity to distil detailed information into concise, actionable insights will provide a significant advantage. For example, a consulting team working with a retail company might use data to inform decisions about store layout and product placement. They may analyse sales data and customer foot traffic to identify trends and patterns, using that information to recommend optimising the store's design.

Seek out diverse perspectives

It is essential to seek out diverse perspectives and to consider multiple viewpoints. You can develop more innovative and effective solutions by working with a diverse team and seeking input from various stakeholders. For example, if you are working with a client to develop a new business strategy, you might seek information from senior executives, frontline employees, customers, and industry experts. By considering the perspectives of these different stakeholders, you can develop a more comprehensive understanding of the business environment and identify new growth opportunities.

Challenge assumptions and biases

Approach problems with an open and objective mindset. Consultants must be able to identify and address their own biases and those of their clients to arrive at the best possible solutions. For example, a consulting team working with a financial services company might challenge assumptions about the value of specific products or services or the behaviour of certain customer segments. By challenging these assumptions, the team can develop a more nuanced understanding of the market and develop more effective strategies.

The ability to think critically and solve problems is vital for consultants. By cultivating a systematic problem-solving approach, posing relevant questions, relying on data for informed decision-making, embracing diverse perspectives, and questioning assumptions and biases, consultants can enhance their capacity to analyse intricate issues and devise impactful solutions. These skills are crucial for excelling in the field of consulting. Consultants can sharpen their skills through hands-on experience, mentorship, and ongoing personal growth focused on nurturing these valuable superhero-like abilities.

"Change is not merely necessary to life — it is life."

Alvin Toffler

4.0 Advancement

Consulting is a fast-paced and dynamic industry that offers a variety of career advancement opportunities for those willing to work hard and take on new challenges. You'll need to have the endurance of a marathon runner, a chess grandmaster's strategic mind, and a seasoned politician's people skills. Above all, it's crucial to maintain a positive attitude, show initiative, and be a team player to gain the trust and respect of your colleagues. Ultimately, advancing in your organisation requires persistence, determination and a willingness to learn and grow.

Build strong relationships
Relationships are key in the consulting world, so building strong relationships with your colleagues, clients, and other stakeholders is paramount. It can mean being proactive about networking, being a team player, and developing a reputation for being reliable and trustworthy.

Demonstrate your expertise

Consulting firms value expertise and knowledge, so staying up-to-date with your field's latest trends and developments is essential. Consider attending industry events, reading thought leadership articles, and staying on top of new technologies and techniques.

Take on new challenges

Consulting is a field that thrives on innovation and problem-solving, so it's vital to be willing to take on new challenges and push yourself outside of your comfort zone. For example, you can take on a new project, a new client, or volunteer to lead a new initiative or team.

Seek out feedback

Feedback is crucial for personal and professional growth as it can help you identify areas for improvement and build on your strengths. Regularly seek feedback from your colleagues, clients, and managers to gain different perspectives on your performance and areas of improvement.

Develop a personal brand

In today's competitive consulting landscape, standing out from the crowd is essential. Developing a personal brand can help you differentiate yourself from other consultants and build a reputation as an expert in your field. First, it will require identifying what you want to be known for. Second, you'll need to consider the appropriate channels, including publishing thought leadership articles, speaking at industry events, or building an online presence. Third, you'll need consistent messaging to build a network of professionals with similar interests.

Build a robust support system

Consulting can be challenging and demanding, so building a solid support system will help you navigate your career's ups and downs. Build relationships with colleagues, join professional organisations, or seek a mentor or coach to help you maintain perspective.

Manage your trajectory

At times in your career, you may find yourself in a role that is not the right fit for you or does not align with your career goals. Discussing your options with your mentor and people manager is essential if this happens. There is no shame in exploring new opportunities within your current firm or elsewhere, especially if it allows you to progress faster in your career.

Advancing within a consulting organisation requires a combination of hard work, dedication, and strategic planning. By building relationships, demonstrating your expertise, taking on new challenges, seeking feedback, being proactive about your career, developing a personal brand, and creating a robust support system, you can position yourself for success and achieve your professional goals.

4.1 People Manager

In most consulting organisations, especially the larger ones, you will be assigned and represented by a "people manager" or "career coach". You will be the Padawan learner and apprentice to these consulting Jedi masters. However, instead of fighting the Empire, you will be fighting to achieve your objectives and get on track for promotion. It is worth remembering that your people manager will be representing you in a moderation process, so developing a positive relationship will be essential. However, if they are disinterested or ineffective, you may seek to be reassigned to someone better aligned with your ambitions.

Figure out the process

Each organisation will have a slightly different consultant performance calibration or moderation approach. It typically occurs once or twice a year and involves each consultant's performance being evaluated compared to others at their grade level. Figure out how this process works within your organisation and plan accordingly.

Understand the performance indicators

Consultant performance is typically measured based on grade-level objectives such as the number of billable hours, sales contribution, and ancillary contributions. Talk to your people manager about what these are at your grade level and how to best go about exceeding them.

Develop a plan

Establish a plan detailing how you will achieve your objectives and work with your people manager to refine it. You should tailor the plan to your specific needs and include actionable steps that you can take to improve your skills and advance your career. Keep track of your performance and take corrective action when required.

Take action

Ultimately, the success of your career will depend on how proactive and determined you are in guiding your career path. You can't wait for things to happen; you must make them happen. Be it joining a specific project, attending networking events, seeking out new opportunities, or expanding your knowledge, you are in control.

Measure progress

Regularly measuring your progress is vital to working with your people manager. It can involve tracking your performance metrics, documenting your achievements, or evaluating your networking success. You can identify improvement areas and adjust your plan by measuring your progress. It can also help you stay motivated and focused on achieving your goals.

Gather feedback

Feedback can help you identify areas where you need to improve and can provide you with actionable steps to enhance your skills. Ask your project leaders, colleagues and clients to provide written feedback on your performance. The feedback you receive will help you and your people manager better understand your contributions and areas for improvement.

Connect regularly

Remember that people managers are only human. They will have their own careers, lives and potentially numerous other colleagues looking to them for advice. It's your opportunity to take the initiative and set up regularly scheduled sessions to connect, review your progress, and receive guidance.

People managers play a critical role in consulting organisations. They will represent you in moderation sessions and may be the difference between securing a promotion and disappointment. It's vital to foster a positive relationship and make their lives easier by developing a plan, tracking progress, and gathering feedback to allow them to tell a compelling story on your behalf.

4.2 Moderation

Some organisations call it calibration, others call it moderation, but whatever the evaluation process is called within your organisation, there is only one word to describe it honestly: terrifying. The process typically occurs once or twice a year, when every consultant is evaluated and ranked. All of your hard work, the contributions you've made, and the feedback you've received will be presented in front of a panel by your people manager and compared to others at your grade level. It's a scary time for all involved, but there are ways you can improve your chances of a favourable outcome.

Grade-level objectives

First and most importantly, you'll need to achieve and ideally exceed your grade-level objectives. Setting clear goals, developing a plan to achieve them, and regularly monitoring progress is essential. Typically your utilisation or billable hour percentage targets and business development contributions will be the most significant performance indicators considered in the process.

Ancillary contributions

In addition to grade-level objectives, there may be other contributions taken into account, such as actions undertaken for the betterment of the organisation, personal development, and the development of others. These contributions can differentiate individuals in situations where their utilisation and business development contributions are similar.

Strong network

Regardless of industry or focus area, it always helps when people know about you before going into a moderation session. Building a network takes time and consistency, so ensure you incorporate it as one of your ongoing activities throughout the year.

Personal brand

In addition to knowing who you are, ensure your network knows what you are about and what knowledge or skills you contribute. Go above and beyond, be proactive, and celebrate success when you or your team achieve important milestones or project wins.

Good story

There is little time in moderation to review each contender, so it's helpful to wrap all accomplishments into a compelling story or narrative. Work with your people manager to ensure your story highlights your achievements and differentiates you from others at your grade level.

The moderation season is one of the most nerve-wracking times of the year for all involved. In addition to meeting or exceeding the utilisation, business development, and ancillary contribution targets, consultants and their people managers must develop a compelling story to help them stand out from the crowd. While success is never guaranteed, with a good story, hard work, effective networking, and a cohesive plan, the probability of success is dramatically increased.

"Communication works for those who work at it."

John Powell

5.0 Communication

Effective communication is crucial in any business or personal relationship. Without it, you might as well be trying to play charades with a group of goldfish. As a consultant, your ability to communicate clearly, concisely, and effectively can make or break a project. Communication is about more than just talking; it's about understanding the needs and expectations of the person you're communicating with. Effective communication helps you establish trust, build rapport, and understand your client's needs and concerns.

Be clear and concise
Getting straight to the point is essential when communicating in a business setting. Avoid overly complicated language, and keep your message simple and easy to understand. For example, if you're emailing a colleague about a project, state the purpose of the email in the first sentence, use bullet points to summarise key thoughts, and include a clear call to action.

Listen actively

Listening is just as important as speaking when it comes to effective communication. Make sure to actively listen to your colleagues or clients and ask questions to ensure you understand their perspectives. For example, if you're in a meeting with a client and they express concern about the project timeline, ask follow-up questions to clarify their expectations and devise a solution together.

Use the appropriate channel

Various situations may require different communication channels. For example, a quick question can be addressed through instant messaging, while a detailed proposal may be better suited for an email or in-person meeting. Knowing which communication channel to use can save time and prevent confusion.

Be mindful of nonverbal cues

Communication isn't just about what you say but also about how you say it. Pay attention to your body language, tone of voice, and facial expressions. For example, a confident and assertive tone can demonstrate your expertise and build trust during a negotiation with a potential client.

Follow up

Refrain from assuming that your message has been received and understood. Follow up with colleagues or clients to ensure that there are no lingering questions or concerns. For example, if you've sent a proposal to a potential client, follow up with a phone call or email to confirm they received it and answer any questions they may have.

Effective communication is essential for any successful consultant. By being clear and concise, listening actively, using the appropriate communication channel, being mindful of nonverbal cues, and following up, you can improve your communication skills and build stronger relationships with colleagues and clients.

5.1 Presentations

Effective presentations are the bread and butter of consulting. Sure, you can have all the expertise and knowledge in the world, but if you can't present it in a way that captivates your audience, you might as well be reading them the dictionary. It's like showing up to a first date with a PhD in astrophysics; it may be impressive, but if you can't hold a conversation, you may end up being single for a long, long time. Delivering an effective presentation can be challenging, especially when dealing with complex information and adapting to the varied expectations of your audience.

Know your audience

Understanding your audience's needs, interests, and level of knowledge can help you tailor your message and deliver it in a way that resonates with them. For example, if you are presenting to a technical audience, you may need to go into more detail about the technical aspects of your findings. Conversely, you need to simplify your language and use more relatable examples in front of a non-technical audience.

Have a clear message

Your message should be concise, focused, and easy to understand. It should answer the key questions that your audience has, such as what the problem is, how it affects them, and what the solution is. Be sure to use straightforward language, avoid jargon, and use visuals to help illustrate your points.

Use visuals

Graphs, charts, and diagrams are powerful tools that simplify complicated information, making it easier for your audience to understand. However, it's essential to strike a balance and avoid overloading your slides with too many visuals or text. After all, the last thing you want is for your audience to spend more time reading slides than listening to your message. So, choose your visuals wisely and use them strategically to reinforce your message.

Tell stories

Stories can illustrate key points, create a sense of empathy, and make the information more relatable. For example, when giving a presentation on a new product launch, you could start by telling a story about a customer struggling with a particular pain point the product solves. The story helps the audience remember the key benefits and features of the product long after the presentation is over.

Practice

Just like learning any new skill, giving effective presentations also requires practice. Make sure to rehearse your presentation multiple times before presenting it to your audience. Rehearsing will help you gain confidence in your material and highlight improvement areas. It will also help you manage your time better and deliver your message clearly and concisely. Remember, practice makes perfect, or at least as close to perfect as we can get.

Engage your audience

Keep your audience engaged and interested throughout your presentation by using several tactics. For example, ask thought-provoking questions and encourage discussion to keep them involved. Additionally, anecdotes or stories can help illustrate your points and keep their attention. Body language is also essential, so make eye contact, use gestures, and vary your tone and pace throughout your presentation. Doing so can keep your audience on their toes and prevent them from nodding off into a daydream about their lunch.

Be prepared for questions

Expect your audience to question your findings, recommendations, or methodology. Be ready to answer these questions confidently and knowledgeably. If you do not know the answer, be honest and offer to follow up with the person later. Effective presentation skills are essential for consultants to convey their insights, findings, and recommendations to their colleagues, clients and stakeholders.

Effective presentation skills are essential for consultants to convey their insights, findings, and recommendations to their colleagues, clients, and stakeholders. To give effective presentations, consultants should tailor their message to their audience, use visuals, practise their delivery, engage the audience, and prepare for questions. By following these steps, consultants can make their presentations more engaging and informative, helping them communicate their ideas clearly and confidently. So, if you want to impress your clients and stakeholders, start honing your presentation skills and showcasing your expertise with poise and panache.

5.2 Active listening

You can have all the knowledge and experience in the world, but if you're not actively listening to others, you're just wasting their time and yours. It's like fixing a car without listening to the engine. Sure, you can change the oil and rotate the tires, but you're not fixing anything if you don't hear that weird knocking sound. So, to be a successful consultant, you better sharpen your listening skills, fully concentrate on what someone is saying, strive to understand their perspective, and provide appropriate feedback.

Focus on the speaker
The first step in active listening is to focus on the speaker, giving them your full attention and avoiding distractions. For example, if you're meeting with a client or colleague, you might put your phone on silent and avoid checking your email.

Use verbal and nonverbal cues
Verbal and nonverbal cues can show the speaker you're engaged and interested in their words. For example, you might nod to indicate that you're following along or use phrases like "I understand" or "go on" to encourage the speaker to keep talking.

Avoid interrupting

Interrupting the speaker can make them feel like you're not interested in what they have to say. Instead, wait for natural pauses in the conversation before asking questions or adding your input. For example, if the speaker shares their concerns about a particular project, you might wait for them to finish before asking, "What do you think the biggest challenge will be in addressing these concerns?"

Paraphrase and summarise

Restating and condensing the speaker's points demonstrates comprehension of their viewpoint and aids in resolving any misunderstandings. For instance, upon hearing the client describe their project objectives, you could respond with, "Am I correct in understanding that your primary focus is on boosting sales and enhancing customer experience?"

Ask clarifying questions

Clarifying questions play a vital role in fostering understanding and preventing misunderstandings when engaging with a speaker. You can gain a more comprehensive understanding of their perspective by seeking additional information and insights. For instance, suppose the speaker is discussing a specific process. In that case, you can ask a clarifying question like, "Can you provide a more detailed explanation of how this process works?" By posing this question, you invite the speaker to elaborate and provide a deeper understanding of the steps, components, and intricacies involved in the process.

Active listening is an essential skill in consulting that can help you better understand your client's needs and provide more effective recommendations. By focusing on the speaker, using verbal and nonverbal cues, avoiding interrupting, paraphrasing, and asking clarifying questions, you can establish rapport and build trust with your clients and colleagues, leading to better outcomes for everyone involved.

5.3 Effective meetings

Effectively moderating meetings is crucial for consultants, who often lead meetings with clients or team members. A meeting without clear objectives or structure is like trying to organise a flash mob without a choreographer. You might get a bunch of people in one place, but if they're not all doing the same dance, it's just chaos. Whether it is a brainstorming session, status update, or decision-making meeting, the success of the meeting often depends on the moderator's ability to keep the conversation on track, encourage participation, and drive towards a clear outcome.

Define clear objectives
Before you schedule a meeting, define clear objectives for what you want to accomplish, which will help you stay focused and avoid wasting time on irrelevant topics. For example, suppose you're meeting with a client to discuss a new product launch. In that case, your objectives might be to gather feedback on the product features, discuss pricing and promotion strategies, and set a timeline for implementation.

Prepare an agenda
Once you've defined your objectives, prepare an agenda that outlines the topics you'll cover and the order in which you'll discuss them. Share the agenda with all attendees in advance so they can come prepared and know what to expect. For example, your agenda might include time slots for introductions, a product demo, a Q&A session, and a discussion of the next steps.

Confirm your assumptions
At the start of the meeting, ensure all participants share the same understanding of the desired outcomes and agenda items, helping frame the discussion as a collaborative exercise. For example, you may ask, "Is everyone okay with this agenda?" or "Is there anything else we want to cover?"
Encourage participation

To make the most of your meeting, encourage participation from all attendees. Ask open-ended questions, solicit feedback, and allow everyone to speak. For example, you might ask, "What do you think of the new product features?" or "Can you share any ideas for increasing our market share?"

Stay on track

It's easy for meetings to get derailed by off-topic discussions or tangents. To stay on track, assign a time limit to each agenda item and stick to it. If a discussion starts to go off track, gently redirect the conversation back to the agenda. For example, you might say, "That's an interesting point, but let's table that discussion for now and focus on the next agenda item."

Summarise action items

At the end of the meeting, summarise the discussed action items and assign ownership to each item to ensure everyone is on the same page and knows what to do next. For example, you might say, "To summarise, John will work on finalising the pricing strategy, Mary will prepare the promotion plan, and I'll follow up with the client to schedule a follow-up call." If appropriate, you may also send a follow-up email with key meeting notes and actions.

Effective meeting moderation is a crucial skill for consultants and can lead to more productive and successful meetings. By setting clear objectives, establishing ground rules, encouraging participation, keeping the conversation on track, summarising, and following up, consultants can ensure their meetings are efficient, productive, and meaningful.

5.4 Structure

You can have all the brains in the world, but if you can't communicate your ideas clearly, you might as well be speaking gibberish. So, to be a successful consultant, you better sharpen those communication skills and get ready to use structured frameworks and concise bullet points like they're going out of style. Effective communication involves articulating your ideas and recommendations clearly by structuring communication in a way that is easy to follow and understand.

Start with a clear objective

Before you start communicating, ensure you have a clear objective. What do you want your audience to know or do? What action do you want them to take? Having a clear purpose will help you stay on track and avoid tangents that can confuse your audience.

Apply a logical structure

When presenting your ideas or data, organise them in a logical structure. Use headings, subheadings, and bullet points to break down your message into easily digestible chunks. It will make it easier for your audience to follow your argument and understand your main points.

Include visuals

Visuals can be a powerful way to support your message and make complex ideas more accessible. Use graphs, charts, and diagrams to illustrate your data and help your audience visualise your argument. Just be sure to keep your visuals easy to read and simple to avoid overwhelming your audience with too much information.

Provide context

When presenting your ideas or data, providing context and background information is vital to helping your audience understand the bigger picture.

The context might include industry trends, historical data, or other relevant information that can help your audience understand the significance of your message.

Summarise key points

Reinforce your message and ensure your audience comprehends your main takeaways by summarising your key points at the end of your presentation or communication. Summarising will also aid in their retention of your message and increase the likelihood of them taking action on it later.

Use plain language

When conveying intricate concepts or presenting data, it is crucial to employ plain language that promotes comprehension. Steer clear of technical jargon or complex terminology that can bewilder your audience. Instead, opt for straightforward, easily understandable language that resonates with everyone. For instance, when discussing a scientific study, you might say, "The researchers discovered that exercise improves heart health," rather than using complex medical terminology. Using straightforward language ensures your message is accessible and effectively communicated to a broader range of people, fostering better understanding and engagement.

Be concise

Finally, be concise in your communication. Stick to the point and avoid rambling or going off on tangents. Remember, your audience's attention span is limited, so make every word count.

Effective communication is essential in consulting, and structured communication ensures that your message is understood and acted upon. Following these tips and examples can improve your communication skills and help you become a more effective consultant.

5.5 Models

Have you ever heard of the Pyramid Principle? No, it's not a new way of building pyramids in Egypt. It's a model by which complex problems or ideas can be broken down into logical elements. Effective communication is critical in consulting, where the ability to convey complex information clearly and succinctly is essential. Consulting firms use a variety of structured communication models to ensure that their recommendations are understood and acted upon.

Pyramid Principle

The Pyramid Principle is a communication framework emphasising structuring information logically and concisely to enhance clarity and comprehension. At its core, the Pyramid Principle suggests that ideas should be presented in a hierarchical structure with a single central point at the top, supported by a few sub-points, and further elaborated upon with specific details and evidence. For example, a consultant may use it to present a strategic recommendation by starting with a central point supported by sub-points and specific details. This approach ensures that the audience can quickly grasp the main message and follow a logical flow of thought.

MECE principle

The MECE principle, an acronym for "Mutually Exclusive, Collectively Exhaustive," is a methodological framework consultants use to structure their thinking and analysis in a clear and organised manner. It dictates that information should be categorised into segments that do not overlap (mutually exclusive) and, when taken together, cover all possible scenarios (collectively exhaustive). For instance, a consultant conducting a market analysis might divide the market into segments based on age groups: children, teenagers, adults, and seniors. This MECE approach ensures that each segment is distinct without any age overlap while also covering the entire spectrum of the market, leaving no age group unaccounted for in the analysis.

Gantt chart

A Gantt chart is a bar chart commonly used in project management consulting to illustrate project schedules and timelines. The chart shows tasks on the vertical axis and time on the horizontal axis. Each task is represented by a bar that shows its duration and start and end dates. Gantt charts can help keep track of project progress and identify potential issues or delays. For example, a consultant might use a Gantt chart to illustrate the timeline for a product launch. The chart might show that specific tasks, such as product testing and packaging design, are taking longer than expected, which could delay the launch date.

SWOT analysis

This structured communication model is often used in business consulting to assess a company's current situation and identify potential areas for improvement. For instance, a consultant might conduct a SWOT analysis for a company struggling to attract new customers. The analysis might reveal that the company has a strong reputation and loyal customer base (Strengths) but an insufficient digital presence (Weaknesses). They may also face increased competition from newer, more innovative competitors (Threats). Based on this information, the consultant might recommend the company invest in improving its digital platforms or fresh marketing strategies to attract a wider audience (Opportunities).

Mind map

A mind map is a visual tool that is used to organise ideas and information in a non-linear way. It typically involves creating a central idea or theme and branching out to related ideas and concepts. Mind maps can be helpful in brainstorming, problem-solving, and strategic planning. For example, a consultant might use a mind map to explore potential marketing strategies for a new product. The central theme might be the product, with branches for the target audience, messaging, and distribution channels.

Fishbone diagram

A fishbone diagram, also known as an Ishikawa diagram, is a visual tool used to identify the root cause of a problem or issue. The diagram resembles a fish skeleton, with the problem or issue at the head and the potential causes branching out from the spine. Fishbone diagrams can help identify a problem's underlying causes and develop practical solutions. For example, a consultant might use a fishbone diagram to identify the causes of low employee morale in a company. The diagram might show that the leading causes are poor management, a lack of training opportunities, and low pay.

Structured communication models or frameworks can aid in presenting complex information clearly and concisely. As a consultant, you will be challenged to identify the most efficient methods to convey information. The aforementioned examples are just a few of the available structured communication models. By utilising these models and others, you will enhance your ability to communicate effectively, help clients make informed decisions, and develop successful strategies.

"If we don't understand people, we don't understand business."

Simon Sinek

6.0 Empathy

Empathy in consulting is like the secret sauce on a burger; you can't have one without the other. Without empathy, you're just a robot spitting out recommendations and strategies devoid of any human connection. You'll need to be able to put yourself in the shoes of others, striving to comprehend their needs, fears, and desires. When you show that you care and are not just there to collect a paycheck, your clients will respond with trust and loyalty. Consultants are expected to be analytical, strategic, and results-oriented, but empathising with people and understanding their unique challenges and perspectives is equally essential.

Listen actively

The Greek Stoic philosopher Epictetus once stated, "We have two ears and one mouth so that we can listen twice as much as we speak." Active listening is the first step towards empathy. It involves paying attention to what others are saying and trying to understand their perspective without judgement, which helps to build trust and rapport with colleagues and clients.

Put yourself in their shoes

Empathy requires you to step outside of your own perspective and consider the perspective of others. Imagine how the other person feels and what they are going through, as it can help you approach the situation with greater understanding and compassion.

Use nonverbal cues

Nonverbal cues, such as eye contact, facial expressions, and body language, can convey empathy and understanding. Using these cues, you can show that you are engaged in the conversation and care about the other person.

Show compassion

Compassion is the feeling of concern for the suffering or misfortune of others. In business, showing compassion can help build stronger relationships with clients and colleagues. For example, if a colleague is struggling with a personal issue, expressing compassion and offering assistance can help them feel valued and supported.

Practice emotional intelligence

Emotional intelligence is the ability to recognise and manage your emotions and those of others. By developing emotional intelligence, you can better understand the feelings of others and respond in a supportive and empathetic way.

Develop effective solutions

To succeed, consultants must create solutions that address client needs and challenges, demonstrating empathy and taking the time to understand the client's perspective and that of their customers and employees. With this holistic approach, consultants can develop effective, practical, and feasible solutions for the client.

Empathy is crucial in consulting, as it is ultimately a human-centric business. After all, consultants must work with people to solve complex problems. Without empathy, they risk treating their clients and colleagues as mere transactions rather than individuals with unique needs and perspectives. Empathy helps consultants establish trust and build rapport, which are essential for delivering value and cultivating long-term relationships.

6.1 Human-centred

If there's one thing that consultants and robots have in common, it's their love for data and efficiency. But here's the thing: humans aren't always the most logical creatures, and sometimes our emotions and idiosyncrasies can throw a wrench into the most data-driven plans. That's why a human-centred approach is so important. You must rely on more than just spreadsheets and algorithms to understand people's motivations and desires. You have to get in there, talk to them, listen to their complaints, and maybe even share a few laughs. Otherwise, you'll end up with a plan that looks great on paper but falls apart in the face of actual human behaviour.

Design thinking
Design thinking is all about putting humans at the centre of the design process. It involves empathising with the user, defining the problem, ideating solutions, prototyping, and testing. Design thinking is a human-centred approach that seeks to create solutions that meet the needs of people. It is a collaborative and iterative process that encourages creativity and innovation. By using design thinking, consultants can develop products and services that are not only functional but also delightful and meaningful for users. A design thinking approach applies to various areas, including product, service, and organisational design.

Personas

User personas are fictional characters that represent different user types. They help businesses understand their audience better and create solutions that meet their needs. For example, let's say a company is developing a mobile app for fitness enthusiasts. To create user personas, they might conduct research and identify three different types of users: "Gym-goer Gary", "Busy Bee Brenda", and "Fitness Fanatic Fran". Gary is a middle-aged man who works out at the gym regularly but struggles to stay motivated. Brenda is a working mom who wants to stay fit but has limited time. Fran is a young athlete who is always looking for new challenges. By creating personas for these different user types, the company can better understand their needs and behaviours to create a mobile app that meets their specific needs.

Customer journey maps

Mapping user journeys involves creating a visual representation of the user experience from start to finish. It helps consultants and businesses identify pain points and opportunities for improvement. For example, let's say a company is redesigning its e-commerce website. To map the user journey, they start with the homepage and create a flowchart showing the user's path from browsing products to purchasing. Along the way, they might identify potential roadblocks or pain points, such as a confusing checkout process or slow loading times. By mapping the user journey, the company can better understand the user's experience and make necessary improvements to create a more seamless and enjoyable shopping experience.

You can't just rely on charts and graphs to understand what makes people tick. Data and efficiency alone cannot capture the idiosyncrasies of human behaviour. Design thinking puts humans at the centre of the design process, leading to collaborative and iterative solutions. User personas and journey maps are essential in this process, helping businesses understand their audience and create solutions that meet their needs. Using a human-centred approach, consultants can develop products and services that function well and resonate with their users.

"I've missed more than 9,000 shots in my career. I've lost almost 300 games. Twenty-six times, I've been trusted to take the game winning shot and missed. I've failed over and over and over again in my life. And that is why I succeed."

Michael Jordan

7.0 Adversity

As a consultant, you're bound to encounter adversity in many forms. Whether it's a difficult client, a complex problem, or a stubborn Excel spreadsheet, the challenges can feel overwhelming at times. But, as the saying goes, when life gives you lemons, you make lemonade. The key to success is embracing adversity, learning from it, and using it as a stepping stone to growth and success.

Take responsibility
Assume accountability for errors or shortcomings, don't blame others or external circumstances, and embrace these moments as opportunities for introspection, considering what went wrong and how you might have approached things differently. Suppose a project fell short due to insufficient communication. In that case, contemplate how you could have fostered more effective communication and apply those insights to future endeavours.

Stay positive

Staying positive and resilient in the face of adversity requires a mindful approach. Maintain a positive mindset by focusing on what you can control. Embrace failures as learning opportunities, and cultivate gratitude for the positives in your life. Finally, surround yourself with a supportive network of friends and mentors who can provide encouragement and guidance.

Keep learning

Continued learning and skill-building are essential to succeeding in consulting. Take courses, attend training sessions, and read industry publications to keep up with the latest trends and best practices. For instance, if a project failed because you lacked specific skills, focus on developing those skills and ensuring you are adequately equipped for future projects.

Embrace collaboration

Consulting is a team sport, and collaboration is critical to success. Leverage your team's strengths and work collaboratively to overcome obstacles and achieve your goals. For example, if a project fails due to a lack of teamwork, reflect on ways to promote collaboration in the future, such as improving communication and encouraging more team-building activities.

Focus on the bigger picture

It's easy to get caught up in the details and lose sight of the bigger picture. When faced with setbacks and failures, take a step back and look at the bigger picture. Reflect on your long-term goals and how this setback fits into your overall journey. Use this as an opportunity to recalibrate and move forward with renewed focus and energy.

Facing setbacks and failures is an inevitable aspect of consulting. However, it is possible to turn these challenges into opportunities for growth and success. The crucial factors to overcome such obstacles include taking responsibility, seeking feedback, maintaining a positive and resilient attitude, continuing to learn, embracing collaboration, and keeping sight of the bigger picture.

It's not about trying to avoid failure altogether but how you respond to it, which can make all the difference in your career. Therefore, when encountering setbacks and failure, take a deep breath, put on your problem-solving hat, and view it as an opportunity to learn and grow.

7.1 Pressure

Dealing with pressure is like trying to defuse a bomb while wearing oven mitts. It's hot, it's stressful, and if you make one wrong move, things could explode in your face. Pressure is a constant companion in the consulting world, with a seemingly endless barrage of tight deadlines, infuriating colleagues, complex projects, and demanding clients. It can lead to stress, burnout, and even mental health issues if not appropriately managed. As the saying goes, a diamond is a chunk of coal that did well under pressure. So, take care of yourself and get ready to shine.

Set boundaries
One of the biggest challenges in consulting is maintaining a healthy work-life balance. Setting boundaries and prioritising time for yourself, your family, and your hobbies is essential. You can do this by setting clear expectations with your clients and colleagues about your availability and taking time off when needed.

Prioritise self-care
It's easy to neglect self-care, such as exercise, sleep, and healthy eating, when under pressure. However, taking care of yourself is crucial for maintaining the energy and focus needed to succeed in consulting. For example, taking a 30-minute walk daily during a particularly stressful project can help clear your head and improve your mood.

Manage time effectively

Manage your time effectively by prioritising tasks based on their importance and urgency, establishing clear goals and deadlines, and developing a system for tracking your progress. Time management tools like calendars, to-do lists, and project management software can also be incredibly helpful in keeping you on track.

Practice mindfulness

Incorporating mindfulness into your routine can be immensely beneficial for staying present, reducing stress, and enhancing focus. For instance, taking a brief break from work to close your eyes and concentrate on your breath is a simple yet effective way to practice mindfulness. This practice lets you clear your mind, replenish your energy, and approach your tasks with renewed clarity and attentiveness. Meditation, yoga, or other mindfulness-based stress reduction techniques can further cultivate mindfulness in your daily life.

Seek support

Consulting firms often provide valuable resources like Employee Assistance Programs (EAPs) to support their employees with various issues, including mental health concerns. These programs offer confidential counselling services and support. Remember, there is no shame in seeking help when you need it. Opening up and reaching out to others can provide valuable perspectives, guidance, and a sense of solidarity during challenging times.

Build a network

Consulting can be stressful and isolating, so building a support network of colleagues, mentors, and friends who can offer advice, encouragement, and support is essential. Maintaining open and honest communication with these individuals is crucial, and being clear about the help you need is vital. It's also helpful to establish a routine of regular check-ins, whether that's through phone calls, video chats, or in-person meetings.

Maintain perspective

Maintaining perspective is crucial to managing stress and preventing burnout. One practical approach is to take a step back and assess the broader context. While consulting projects can be all-consuming, it's essential to remember that they represent only a fraction of the overall business, industry landscape, or our lives. Putting things into perspective helps us realise that challenges, no matter how daunting, may not be as overwhelming as they initially appear.

Dealing with pressure in consulting is an ongoing challenge that requires a proactive approach to managing stress and maintaining a healthy work-life balance. By setting boundaries, prioritising self-care, managing time effectively, practising mindfulness, seeking support, building a support network, and maintaining perspective, you can develop the resilience and skills needed to succeed in this fast-paced and demanding industry.

7.2 Travel

It's like playing a game of travel roulette. You never know if you'll end up in first-class luxury or cramped in coach beside a snoring passenger. One day you're flying high with a window seat and a glass of champagne, and the next day you're stuck in the middle seat between two people who seem to have taken over the armrests. Despite the challenges, there's something exhilarating about travelling as a consultant. It's a chance to see new places, meet new people, and experience new things. Just be prepared for the unexpected, and remember to pack your sense of humour.

Plan ahead

Before travelling, ensure you have all the necessary documents, including your passport, travel visa, and any required work permits. Research your destination to learn about local customs, currency, and transportation options. Make a packing list, and be sure to include any necessary business attire.

Stay connected

Pack all the technology you need to stay connected while on the road, including a reliable laptop, smartphone, and charger. Ensure you can access email, messaging, and other communication tools to stay in touch with clients, colleagues, and partners.

Pack smart

When packing for a business trip, only bring what you need and pack as efficiently as possible. Try to keep it simple. If you're travelling for an extended period, consider packing essential items that can be mixed and matched to create different outfits. Of course, remember to pack any necessary medications, toiletries, and other personal items.

Be flexible

Delays and unexpected changes can and will happen, so building in extra buffer time is important whenever possible. It could mean booking an earlier flight or arriving at your destination a day in advance. Being flexible means having a backup plan in case something goes wrong, whether it's a flight cancellation or a sudden change in your schedule.

Stay healthy

Travel can take a toll on your health, so take care of yourself while on the road. Consider packing healthy snacks to keep your energy levels up throughout the day. Stay hydrated, get plenty of rest, take advantage of the hotel gym, avoid the bar, and eat healthy meals whenever possible.

Stay organised

Keep all your travel documents and itinerary in one place, and ensure you have easy access to them when needed. Use a travel wallet or folder to keep everything organised and your receipts and expense reports up to date. Additionally, remember to enrol in any and all hotel or airline loyalty programmes to accrue reward points, as you may be able to use them on your trips down the line.

Enjoy the experience
Travelling as a consultant can be a unique opportunity to experience new places and cultures. Take advantage of any free time you have. If you can, don't hesitate to add an additional day or two to your itinerary to explore the local area, try new foods, or meet new people. Taking time for yourself can make your trip more enjoyable and provide valuable insights and inspiration for your work.

Following these tips can help ensure a successful and stress-free travel experience. Remember to plan ahead, stay connected, pack smart, be flexible, stay healthy, stay organised, and take advantage of the experience. With some preparation and a positive attitude, you can make the most of your time on the road.

7.3 Vices

Vices can be a real pain in the butt, or rather, in the lungs, liver, and waistline, especially if you're addicted to something as innocent as eating cupcakes. One minute you're nibbling on a delicious treat, and the next, you're shoving a whole dozen in your mouth while hiding under your desk. Dealing with vices can be a challenge for anyone, but it can be especially difficult in the high-pressure environment of the consulting industry. The long hours, constant travel, and demanding clients can make it easy to fall into the trap of using alcohol, drugs, or other destructive behaviours as a way to cope.

Acknowledge the problem
Acknowledging that you have a problem can be a challenging and uncomfortable experience, but it's the first step towards recovery. It takes courage and honesty to admit that your behaviours may be hurting yourself or others, and it can be humbling to realise that you don't have complete control. Remember, seeking help is a sign of strength, not weakness, and it's never too late to start making positive changes in your life.

Seek help

When dealing with vices, seeking help and support from professionals, friends, or family is crucial. There are many resources available for individuals struggling with addiction or harmful behaviours, such as support groups and counselling services. Remember, you don't have to do it alone.

Create a support system

It's essential to have people in your life who understand what you're going through and are willing to support you in your journey, including family, friends, support groups, or a therapist. Be open and honest with your support system about your struggles, and communicate what kind of help you need. They can provide encouragement, offer practical advice, and hold you accountable.

Identify healthy coping mechanisms

Find positive and constructive ways to manage stress and emotions that don't involve turning to your vice. Healthy coping mechanisms may include exercise, meditation, therapy, talking to a trusted friend or family member, journaling, or engaging in a favourite hobby. You can develop a healthier and more fulfilling lifestyle by replacing negative habits with positive ones.

Hold yourself accountable

Take responsibility for your actions and acknowledge when you slip up. Be honest with yourself and avoid making excuses or justifications for your behaviour. One way to hold yourself accountable is to track your progress towards your goals and evaluate your success regularly.

Set goals

Start by identifying the specific behaviours you want to change, such as reducing alcohol consumption or quitting smoking. Then, set realistic and measurable goals, such as reducing your alcohol intake to a certain number of drinks per week or quitting smoking within a specific timeframe. It can be helpful to break down larger goals into smaller, achievable steps.

Celebrate progress

Celebrating success can be as simple as giving yourself a pat on the back, treating yourself to something you enjoy, or sharing your accomplishments with others who have supported you along the way. Recognising your successes can help boost your motivation and confidence, reminding you that you are capable of achieving your goals.

It's essential to remember that dealing with vices is a journey, and you should be patient and kind to yourself throughout the process. You can take control of your life and overcome your vices by acknowledging the problem, seeking help, setting goals, creating a support system, finding healthy coping mechanisms, holding yourself accountable, and celebrating progress. By doing so, you can gradually build a healthier, more productive, and fulfilling career. So, don't be too hard on yourself, and focus on making progress, one step at a time.

7.4 Redundancy

The consulting industry can be ruthless and volatile, which means there may come a time when you're asked to leave your role. It's the professional equivalent of a breakup. You thought everything was going great, but to your surprise, you received a termination notice and a separation package. Just like in a breakup, you're left confused, angry, and slightly relieved that you no longer have to deal with the drama. So take a deep breath, a quick nap, and prepare for the next chapter of your professional life.

Take time to process

Losing your job can be an emotional experience, so take some time to process your feelings before jumping into job searching or networking. Talk to friends and family, practice self-care, and take some time to reflect on what you want for your career moving forward.

Seek support

Reach out to family, friends, and professional support services such as career coaches or mental health professionals to help you cope with the stress and uncertainty of redundancy.

Don't burn bridges

Even if you were fired in a less-than-ideal situation, it's essential to remain professional and not burn bridges with your former employer. You never know when you might need a reference or recommendation, so make sure to leave on good terms.

Understand your rights

Make sure you understand your rights regarding redundancy, including your severance package and entitlements such as unemployment benefits.

Update your resume

Take some time to reflect on your experiences and accomplishments in your previous role and highlight them on your resume and LinkedIn profile.

Network and job search

Reach out to your professional network and let them know you're looking for new opportunities. Attend networking events, job fairs, and industry conferences to expand your connections and job prospects.

Stay positive

Being let go is a devastating experience, but it's essential to stay positive and optimistic about the future. Remember that it does not define your worth as a person or a professional. While transitioning to a new role may take time, don't get discouraged. Use the time to be productive, get to the gym, eat right, catch up with friends or go for a walk. Stay optimistic and keep pushing forward towards your goals.

It's essential to remember that setbacks can happen to even the most successful people. Take the example of Steve Jobs, who was famously fired from the very company he co-founded. Rather than giving up, he channelled the experience into fueling his passion for innovation and established a new venture, NeXT. Eventually, he was rehired by Apple and became one of the most successful and influential figures in the tech industry. While we may not all be Steve Jobs, we can learn from his resilience and use our setbacks as opportunities for growth and success.

"I never lose. I either win or I learn."

Nelson Mandela

8.0 Selling

Selling consulting services requires a certain finesse. You can't just barge into a client's office and pitch your services like a used car salesperson. If you try to sweet talk a potential client with lines like "This consulting package is a real steal", they might not take you seriously. Instead, you must understand their needs, build trust and credibility, and develop a tailored proposal. It can be daunting, especially if you are unfamiliar with the sales process.

Understand your client's needs
Before pitching your consulting services, take the time to understand your client's needs and challenges. Identifying their pain points, goals, and objectives will enable you to customise your pitch to precisely meet their specific requirements and increase the likelihood of a successful engagement.

Follow the process
Consulting organisations typically have well-defined procedures for qualifying opportunities, determining pricing, and obtaining approvals.

It is crucial to comprehend the entire process, identify the key stakeholders, understand the requirements, and be aware of the timelines associated with each phase. If any uncertainties arise, it is important to proactively seek clarification and obtain the necessary answers instead of relying on assumptions.

Articulate your value proposition

Differentiate yourself from competitors through your unique value proposition. Showcase your team's skills and expertise, and outline how you will help clients achieve their goals. Be clear and concise, focusing on the benefits your services provide.

Build trust and credibility

Building trust and credibility is crucial in consulting engagements. To accomplish this, present case studies and references that showcase your track record of success. Demonstrate how your services have delivered positive outcomes for previous clients.

Develop a tailored proposal

Once you understand your client's needs, develop a tailored proposal outlining the scope of work, timelines, deliverables, and pricing. Be specific about your services and how they will benefit your client.

Follow up and stay engaged

Address client questions and concerns proactively after submitting your proposal. Stay available during the engagement to build lasting relationships and increase the probability of winning future opportunities.

Overall, selling consulting services requires a combination of understanding your client's needs, articulating your value proposition, building trust and credibility, developing a tailored proposal, and following up and staying engaged. Following these tips can help you effectively sell your consulting services and help your clients achieve their goals.

8.1 RFPs

A Request for Proposal (RFP) is a formal document that outlines the needs and requirements of a potential client and invites vendors to submit proposals that meet those needs. You'll spend hours poring over documents, assembling a team of experts, and crafting the perfect proposal. Inevitably, just when you think you've finally completed the document, you get a notification that the deadline has been extended because, apparently, the client enjoys watching you suffer. So, take a deep breath, grit your teeth, and try to keep your sense of humour, knowing that the only way out is through.

Understand the requirements

The first step is to understand the requirements outlined in the document, including identifying the client's needs, goals, expectations, and any specific instructions or guidelines for the proposal. For example, if the RFP requires a particular format or structure, make sure to adhere to those guidelines. Understanding the requirements will help you tailor your proposal to the client's needs and increase your chances of winning the business.

Qualify the opportunity

Evaluate if the project aligns with your business objectives, if you have the necessary resources and expertise to deliver on the requirements, and if the project is profitable. Responding to an RFP without proper qualification can lead to wasted time and resources. It may result in a proposal not tailored to the client's needs or not aligning with your organisation's capabilities.

Bring together a team

An RFP response is a time-consuming process that requires multiple inputs and a significant amount of effort. It is not a task that you should take on alone, so it's essential to assemble a team with the appropriate skills, experience, and availability to work on the proposal from start to finish. Collaborating with a team ensures that all aspects of the proposal are considered and that the final product meets the client's requirements.

Plan ahead

Drafting an effective RFP response is a project in its own right. To ensure a successful submission, develop a project plan considering the significant milestones, internal checks, revisions, and approvals required. Use a structured approach such as backward planning, considering the submission deadline, and including ample buffer time to avoid last-minute drama.

Ask questions

It's common for clients to organise a call or question submission process to clarify any aspects of the RFP. Ensure you clearly understand the requirements by reviewing the RFP in detail, gathering questions from all team members, and submitting them to address any ambiguous elements. By submitting questions, you can demonstrate your organisation's interest in the project, gain additional information that may not have been initially provided, and ensure that your proposal addresses all requirements.

Develop a clear and concise proposal

Clients are busy and don't have time to read through lengthy proposals filled with irrelevant information. Your submission should be clear, concise, and focused on addressing the client's needs. Use a clear structure with headers, subheadings, and bullet points to make your proposal easy to skim and understand. Provide specific examples and case studies to demonstrate your experience and expertise.

Be competitive with your pricing

Pricing is an essential factor for clients when choosing a vendor. Your proposal should include a competitive pricing structure aligned with the project's scope and requirements. Be transparent about your pricing and provide a detailed breakdown of the costs. For example, if the RFP requires a pricing table, provide a clear and detailed breakdown of all costs involved, payment milestones, and associated deliverables, including any additional fees or charges.

Articulate assumptions and restrictions

Ambiguity is not your friend, especially when submitting complex proposals. Assumptions are statements that outline specific conditions that are not explicitly stated in the RFP but are assumed to be true. Restrictive language, on the other hand, sets boundaries and limitations on the proposal's scope. By including assumptions and restrictive language, consultants can ensure that the client understands the scope and limitations of their proposal, reducing the risk of miscommunication and disputes later in the project.

Follow up

Following up with the client after submitting your proposal is crucial to confirm its receipt and address any questions they may have. It's vital to remain available throughout the evaluation process to handle any concerns or issues that may arise. You may also be asked to provide additional information, make a presentation, answer further questions, or negotiate on specific aspects of the proposal. By being responsive and flexible, you can demonstrate your commitment to the project and improve your chances of winning the bid.

A strategic and detailed approach is essential to achieving a favourable outcome when responding to an RFP. It involves comprehending the client's needs, assembling a proficient team, crafting a clear and succinct proposal, and following up with the client. Each step is crucial in increasing the likelihood of winning the bid and acquiring new business for your organisation. Planning ahead, being competitive with pricing, and articulating assumptions and requirements can enhance your chances of success. It's also important to remain flexible and responsive and to address any challenges or issues that may arise during the process.

8.2 Expectations

Winning a project is like winning the lottery, except you get a million headaches instead of winning a million dollars. It's exciting to land a new project and pop open a bottle of champagne to celebrate, but that's only the beginning. Clients hire consultants to solve complex problems and expect results, which can lead to high expectations and unrealistic demands. Therefore, preparing to manage these expectations effectively is essential. So, while landing a new project can be rewarding, be ready for the headaches that come with it and strive to manage client expectations to ensure a successful project outcome.

Clarify scope and deliverables

One of the essential steps in managing client expectations is to clarify the scope of the project and the deliverables. The consultant must work with the client to understand their goals and objectives and clearly describe the work that will be done, including timelines, milestones, and expected outcomes. For example, in a consulting project focused on developing a new product for a client, the consultant should work with the client to identify the scope of features and functions that the product should include, along with a detailed timeline for delivery and the format of the deliverables.

Set realistic expectations

Setting realistic expectations is critical to managing client expectations effectively. The consultant must be honest with the client about what can and cannot be achieved within the project's scope. Setting unrealistic expectations can lead to the client's disappointment and frustration and damage the consultant's reputation. For example, in a consulting project focused on improving a company's customer service, the consultant should be realistic about the time and resources required to implement changes and their impact on customer satisfaction.

Communicate regularly

Consultants must communicate regularly with the client, providing updates on progress, identifying any issues that arise, and discussing any changes to the project scope or timeline. Never assume that all client stakeholders have the same level of understanding. Regular communication helps to ensure that the client stakeholders remain informed and engaged throughout the project, reducing the risk of misunderstandings or unrealistic expectations. For instance, in a consulting project centred around enhancing an online platform for a client, the consultant should involve client stakeholders in interactive workshop sessions, provide frequent updates on the project's advancement, and promptly address any issues or delays that arise. This open and consistent communication approach fosters transparency, trust, and collaboration between the consultant and the client, enhancing the overall project outcomes.

Manage risks and issues

Risks and issues are inevitable in any consulting project, and it is essential to manage them effectively to avoid surprises that can impact client expectations. It is necessary to identify potential risks and issues early on and develop strategies to mitigate them. For example, in a consulting project focused on implementing a new software system, the project team may identify a risk that the system may not be compatible with existing hardware. To manage this risk, the team may develop a plan to test the system's compatibility before implementation.

Be transparent

Consultants must be transparent about the process, including the approach, methods, and potential risks. They should also be transparent about any limitations or constraints impacting the project's outcomes. For example, in a consulting project focused on improving a company's financial performance, the consultant should be transparent about the limitations of financial forecasting models and the potential impact of external factors such as changes in the market or regulations.

Manage change effectively

Change is inevitable in consulting projects, and managing change effectively is critical to managing client expectations. The consultant must be able to identify potential changes in the project scope or timeline and communicate them to the client as early as possible. The consultant should also work with the client to manage any changes to the project, ensuring that they are incorporated into the project plan and timeline. For example, in a consulting project focused on developing a new marketing strategy for a client, the consultant may need to adjust the strategy based on changes in the market or customer feedback.

In consulting, adeptly managing expectations becomes essential, particularly when clients or partners harbour lofty expectations or make unrealistic demands. Successful consultants navigate this challenge by diligently clarifying project scope and deliverables, maintaining regular and open lines of communication, effectively addressing risks and issues, fostering transparency throughout the process, and skillfully managing change. By mastering these elements, consultants can secure favourable project outcomes while cultivating enduring client relationships.

"A goal without a plan is just a wish."

Antoine de Saint-Exupéry

9.0 Project management

Project management is like being the conductor of an orchestra. Sure, each musician can play their instrument decently on their own, but without someone to lead and coordinate them, it's just a bunch of noise. Effective project management is essential for the success of any project, regardless of its size or complexity. A well-managed project ensures that it is completed on time, within budget, and to the required quality standards. It involves planning, organising, controlling, and monitoring all aspects of the project from start to finish. It also involves identifying and managing risks and issues, communicating with stakeholders, and ensuring that all team members are working towards the same objectives.

Define clear objectives
It is essential to begin by defining specific, measurable, and achievable objectives. Setting clear objectives at the outset ensures that all stakeholders are aligned towards the same goals and that progress can be monitored effectively.

Develop a detailed plan

Once you have clear objectives, it's time to develop a detailed project plan, including timelines, milestones, deliverables, and a clear breakdown of tasks and responsibilities. It's crucial to involve all stakeholders in the planning process to ensure everyone clearly understands the project requirements and timelines.

Assign resources effectively

Identify the resources needed for the project, such as personnel, equipment, and materials, and ensure they are allocated appropriately. It also involves managing these resources throughout the project lifecycle, including monitoring progress and adjusting as needed.

Communicate regularly

Yes, we've mentioned communication numerous times, but it bears repeating. Regular updates and progress reports ensure that everyone involved is aware of the project's status and can take appropriate actions. Communication also enables stakeholders to identify and address issues or potential roadblocks before they become significant risks to the engagement.

Manage risks and issues

Risks and issues are an inevitable part of any project. Effective project management involves proactively identifying and managing these risks, including developing contingency plans for potential issues and monitoring the project closely to identify any emerging risks. By addressing risks and issues proactively, you can minimise their impact on the project and ensure that it stays on track.

Measure and evaluate performance

Finally, effective project management involves measuring and evaluating performance throughout the project lifecycle, including tracking progress against the project plan, assessing the quality of deliverables, gathering feedback from stakeholders, and making adjustments as necessary.

Several key considerations are required to guarantee the success of consulting projects, including defining clear objectives, creating a comprehensive plan, allocating resources efficiently, maintaining regular communication, mitigating risks and addressing issues, and continually monitoring and evaluating performance. It is important to note that effective project management is a continuous process that requires active participation and collaboration from all stakeholders to ensure project success.

9.1 Backward planning

Backward planning is a powerful tool for achieving success in any project, whether in consulting, business, or personal life. Backward planning, also known as reverse planning, is a project management technique that involves starting with the desired outcome or goal and working backwards to determine the steps required to achieve it. It's a structured approach that allows you to identify the tasks, milestones, and deadlines needed to achieve your objective and allocate the necessary resources and time accordingly.

Define the objective
The first step in backward planning is to define the project goal and deliverables. Let's say the project is to launch a new software product. The end goal is to have a functioning software product that meets customer needs and is ready to launch. The final deliverables may include a user-friendly interface, a functional backend, and a marketing campaign to promote the launch.

Identify the critical path
Once the project goal and deliverables have been defined, the next step is identifying the critical path. You'll need to work backwards from the objective, breaking down the project into smaller tasks and determining the dependencies between them. For the software product launch, working backwards, some tasks may include creating marketing materials, testing the software, and developing the software.

Determine the timeline

Establishing the project's end date first makes determining the required duration for each task and allocating resources accordingly easier. This approach helps to mitigate the risk of underestimating the time needed to complete each task. It ensures that the project stays on track. When using backward planning, it is essential to identify any dependencies between tasks and adjust the schedule accordingly. For example, the software development might take four months, the testing might take two weeks, and the marketing campaign might take three months.

Assign tasks

With the timeline in place, the next step is to assign tasks and responsibilities, including identifying who will be responsible for each task and ensuring everyone understands their role and expectations. For example, the front-end development might be assigned to one team member, while the back-end development might be assigned to another team member.

Monitor progress

Once the project is underway, monitoring progress and adjusting as needed are essential. It may involve tracking the completion of each task and comparing it to the timeline. For example, suppose the front-end development is taking longer than expected. In that case, adjustments may need to be made to the resources allocated to ensure the project stays on track.

Backward planning is a powerful tool used in project management to ensure that projects are completed on time and within budget. By starting with the end goal in mind and working backwards, project managers can identify the critical path, determine the timeline, assign tasks and responsibilities, and monitor progress to ensure success. Applying backward planning can lead to more effective project management and successful outcomes.

9.2 Agile

Initially designed for software development, Agile methodology has gained widespread popularity across diverse industries. It presents a flexible and iterative approach that highlights collaboration, ongoing enhancement, and providing value to customers. As a project management approach, Agile methodology underscores adaptability, teamwork, and customer-centricity. It entails breaking down projects into smaller tasks that can be accomplished within short iterations or sprints, enabling teams to adapt to evolving requirements and priorities promptly, and ensuring timely delivery of tangible value.

Define the scope and goals
The first step in an agile business approach is to define the project scope and goals, identify what needs to be accomplished, and set clear objectives. For example, if the project is to develop a new software product, the scope might include creating a user-friendly interface and a functional backend.

Build a cross-functional team
The second step is to build a cross-functional team, bringing together individuals with different skill sets and backgrounds to collaborate on the project. For example, the team might include developers, designers, marketers, and quality assurance specialists.

Develop a backlog
Creating a backlog involves identifying all the tasks that must be completed to achieve the project goals and organising them into a list. For example, the software product backlog might include tasks related to designing elements of the interface, developing the backend components, and testing the software.

Prioritise tasks

Once the backlog has been developed, the next step is prioritising tasks, identifying the most critical tasks, and organising them into sprints. Each sprint is typically two to four weeks long and focuses on completing a subset of the prioritised backlog. For example, the first sprint might focus on tasks related to developing and testing the backend.

Work in sprints

Each sprint focuses on completing the highest priority subset of the backlog, with daily meetings held to discuss progress and identify any roadblocks. For example, during the backend development sprint, the team might hold daily standup meetings to discuss progress and identify any issues that need to be resolved.

Review and adapt

The final step is to review and adapt. At the end of each sprint, the team reviews what was accomplished and identifies any lessons learned. They then use this information to adjust their approach and improve the project. For example, after completing the backend development sprint, the team might review what worked well and what didn't to make adjustments for the next sprint. The team may also add tasks to the backlog and reprioritise them as needed.

An agile business approach is a powerful tool for project management that emphasises flexibility, adaptability, and continuous improvement. By breaking down projects into smaller, more manageable tasks, prioritising them, and working on them in sprints, project managers can ensure that projects are completed efficiently and effectively. An agile business approach can lead to more successful project outcomes and improve business performance.

9.3 Premortem

Project management involves many moving parts; even with the most meticulous planning, things can still go wrong. One tool that project managers can use to anticipate potential problems is the premortem exercise. The premortem is an activity where a project team imagines that the project has failed and then works backwards to identify the causes of that failure. The objective is to proactively recognise and address possible challenges before they occur, foster cooperation, mitigate the likelihood of project setbacks, and establish a blueprint for potential remedies.

Define the project

The first step in a premortem approach is to define the project, identifying the project goals, objectives, and scope. For example, if the project is to launch a new product, the goals may include increasing sales and expanding market share.

Imagine the project failed

This activity asks the team to imagine that the project, platform, or programme has already been launched but failed to meet the set goals and objectives. For example, if the goal was to increase sales, the team might imagine that the product has not sold well and has been discontinued.

Identify reasons for failure

The team should brainstorm all the possible reasons why the project failed. In this case, reasons for failure could include factors such as poor market research, inadequate resources, or ineffective marketing. For example, the team might identify that the product did not meet customer needs, was too expensive, or lacked differentiation from competitors.

Develop solutions

Once the reasons for failure have been identified, the next step is to develop solutions by brainstorming potential solutions to address each identified risk. For example, suppose the team identified a risk that the product did not meet customer needs. In that case, they might develop a plan to conduct additional market research and incorporate customer feedback into the product design.

Implement solutions

The final step is to implement the solutions. The team should prioritise mitigations for the most likely risks and develop plans for implementing them, which may include reallocating resources, adjusting the project scope, or revising the marketing strategy. For example, the team might prioritise market research and customer feedback, allocating additional resources to these areas to ensure that the product meets customer needs.

A premortem approach is a valuable tool for project managers to identify and address potential risks before they become significant issues. By imagining that the project has already failed, specifying the reasons for failure, developing solutions, and implementing them, project managers can ensure that projects are completed efficiently and effectively. It's important to encourage collaboration and prioritise the most likely scenarios to develop a roadmap for potential solutions. Remember, a premortem exercise is not about assigning blame but improving the probability of the project's success.

9.4 Change management

Change management can be a bit like trying to herd cats. Just when you think you've got everything under control, someone wanders in a different direction, and you're left scrambling to bring them back on track. Countless projects have been derailed due to the innate human reluctance to embrace change, regardless of how well-intentioned. Effective change management practices are crucial for easing transitions and promoting collaboration when introducing new technologies, processes, or organisational structures.

Develop a clear vision

Before implementing any change, it's essential to have a clear vision of why it's necessary and how it will benefit the organisation. Communicating a well-defined vision to all affected employees ensures everyone is on the same page. For instance, when General Electric implemented their "Work-Out" programme, they had a clear vision of improving communication and problem-solving throughout the organisation.

Engage stakeholders

Engaging all affected stakeholders is essential to the success of any initiative and may include employees, customers, and suppliers. It's necessary to involve them in the process, listen to their concerns, and address any issues they may have. For example, when United Airlines developed a new ticketing system, they engaged customers to gather feedback and adjust based on their needs.

Communicate effectively

It's critical to communicate the change early and often, using multiple channels to ensure everyone is informed. It's also vital to be transparent about the process, including timelines and potential roadblocks. For instance, when Procter & Gamble implemented a new performance management system, they communicated the change through multiple channels, including town hall meetings and company-wide emails.

Provide training and support

Employees often find change challenging, so it is crucial to offer the requisite training and support to facilitate their adaptation. Providing comprehensive assistance, such as job aids, training resources, and ongoing guidance, is vital for addressing potential concerns. For example, when IBM instituted a new software system, they conducted extensive training sessions to ensure employees felt at ease with the updated technology.

Measure and adjust

It's essential to measure the success of the change management initiative and make adjustments as needed, including gathering employee feedback, monitoring key metrics, and making changes as necessary to ensure the initiative is on track. For instance, when Walmart implemented a new store scheduling system, they gathered employee feedback and adjusted it to ensure it met their needs.

Celebrate success

Finally, it's important to celebrate success and recognise the hard work of everyone engaged in the change management process, which can help build morale and encourage continued success. For example, when Target launched a new store format, they celebrated success with a grand opening event and recognised the hard work of all employees involved.

Effective change management is critical for organisations to stay competitive and adjust to market conditions. Incorporating best practices and drawing inspiration from successful change management initiatives can ensure that all parties accept the changes. With careful planning, thoughtful communication, and a collaborative approach, consulting firms can assist organisations in navigating change, implementing it smoothly, and positioning them for long-term success.

9.5 Engagement

Imagine you walk into a tattoo parlour, excited to get some new ink. But to your horror, you're informed that you have zero control over the design or placement. Sounds like a nightmare, right? That's exactly how it feels for client stakeholders when consultants swoop in, announcing an initiative that could shake up their corner of the organisation. Just like you wouldn't want a random tattoo artist making decisions for you, stakeholders don't want to feel like something is being forced upon them. That's why keeping client stakeholders engaged is crucial for consultants. Engaging stakeholders throughout the project lifecycle ensures collaboration and that their perspectives, insights, and expectations are considered. After all, nobody wants a tattoo they didn't sign up for, just like nobody wants a project forced upon them without their input.

Clear communication

Establishing clear and open lines of communication is vital for engaging client stakeholders. Regularly scheduled meetings, status updates, and progress reports allow stakeholders to stay informed and provide valuable input. For instance, in a project focused on improving organisational processes, consider scheduling weekly check-ins with key stakeholders to discuss progress and gather feedback.

Stakeholder involvement

Involving stakeholders in workshops or collaborative sessions enhances their engagement and fosters a sense of ownership of the project. These sessions can include brainstorming, ideation, and problem-solving exercises. For example, in a marketing strategy project, organise workshops to gather insights from different stakeholders, such as marketing managers, sales representatives, and customer service representatives, enabling them to contribute their expertise and perspectives.

Tailored communication

Recognise that different stakeholders have varying levels of understanding and preferences for receiving information. Tailor your communication and reporting methods to cater to individual stakeholder needs. Some prefer detailed reports, while others respond better to concise summaries or visual presentations. You can effectively engage stakeholders by understanding and adapting to their communication preferences. For instance, in an IT infrastructure project, provide technical reports for IT stakeholders and present executive summaries for C-suite stakeholders.

Active participation

Promote active engagement from stakeholders whom the project will ultimately impact. Encourage their input, actively seek their opinions, and involve them in decision-making. Doing so enhances their level of involvement and ensures that their valuable expertise is utilised to achieve the best possible results. For instance, arrange focus groups with end-users in a product development project, engage them in usability testing, and collect their feedback to drive iterative improvements.

Addressing concerns

Promptly address any concerns or issues raised by stakeholders. Active listening, empathy, and effective problem-solving are vital to managing stakeholder expectations. When stakeholders feel heard and valued, their engagement and commitment to the project are strengthened. For example, in a rebranding project, hold individual meetings with key stakeholders to address any concerns or resistance to change they may not otherwise voice in a group setting, ensuring a smoother transition.

Consultants can foster robust engagement and collaboration by employing clear communication channels, stakeholder involvement, tailored reporting, active participation, and addressing concerns. By prioritising stakeholder engagement, consultants can build strong partnerships, leverage valuable insights, and deliver exceptional results for their clients.

9.6 Escalations

Escalations are like a tornado you did not see coming. Your team may have ignored the first few raindrops and the ominous gathering clouds signalling the storm. Before you know it, the tornado forms overhead, and you're swept up in the dreaded whirlwind of escalations. In the world of consulting, escalations are an inevitable part of the job. They can arise for various reasons, such as client dissatisfaction, project delays, budget constraints, or miscommunication. How well consultants handle these escalations can significantly impact client relationships and project success.

Stay calm

When faced with an escalation, remaining composed and maintaining a positive mindset is essential. Escalations can be stressful, but panicking or becoming defensive will not help the situation. Instead, take a deep breath, remind yourself of your capabilities, and confidently approach the situation. Suppose you receive negative feedback from a client or partner about a deliverable. Rather than becoming discouraged, stay calm, accept the feedback gracefully, and express your willingness to address the concerns.

Seek guidance

Recognising that you are part of a larger team with experienced professionals is crucial. When facing an escalation, don't hesitate to seek guidance and support from senior colleagues. They can provide valuable insights, share past experiences, and guide you on the best course of action. For example, when encountering a complex technical issue during a project, reach out to a senior colleague with expertise in that area. By seeking their advice and collaborating on a solution, you can demonstrate initiative and a commitment to problem-solving.

Identify the underlying cause

When an escalation arises, it is vital to identify the underlying causes rather than simply addressing the surface-level issues. Conduct a thorough analysis to understand the root causes and propose appropriate actions to rectify them. By focusing on the cause, you can prevent similar escalations from recurring. For example, if a project experiences frequent delays due to inadequate resources, propose a revised resource allocation plan, provide the necessary training, or explore outsourcing options.

Define an escalation process

For internal team issues, the escalation process may be as simple as emailing a colleague about the unaddressed issue and adding their manager to the CC, which always prompts a hastened response. For client projects, it's helpful to establish a straightforward escalation process with predefined escalation levels, ensuring that all team members know their roles and responsibilities. Identify key decision-makers and empower them to make necessary decisions swiftly. Communicate the escalation path to clients so they understand whom to contact in case of issues or concerns. For example, during a large-scale transformation project, if a client expresses dissatisfaction with the progress, a predefined escalation path would quickly involve the project manager, who would then engage senior leadership to address the client's concerns.

Establish communication channels

Open lines of communication are the foundation of successful escalation management. Set up regular meetings with stakeholders to address concerns, monitor progress, and manage expectations. Encourage transparent and honest conversations, ensuring that clients feel heard and understood. Actively listen to their concerns and provide timely updates on the project status. For example, suppose a team encounters delays in delivering a key milestone due to technical difficulties.

Instead of avoiding the issue, they proactively communicate the challenges to the client, explain the impact on the project timeline, and propose alternative solutions. By maintaining open communication, trust is built, and the client understands that their needs are being prioritised.

Anticipate risks

Of course, the best types of escalations are the ones that never happen. By anticipating risks, consultants can develop contingency plans and preventive measures to mitigate their impact. This proactive approach, utilising methods such as the premortem exercise, allows for better preparedness and enables swift and effective action when faced with unexpected developments. Whether foreseeing potential delays, client dissatisfaction, or resource constraints, anticipating risks empowers consultants to navigate escalations with agility and minimise their disruptive effects. By considering various scenarios and staying one step ahead, consultants can ensure a smoother escalation process and increase the chances of achieving successful outcomes.

Escalations in consulting can be like a tornado, catching you off guard in the whirlwind. However, you can weather the storm and navigate escalations successfully by staying calm, seeking guidance, identifying underlying causes, establishing an escalation process, maintaining open communication channels, and anticipating the risks involved. Escalations present an opportunity for growth and learning, allowing you to refine your problem-solving skills and strengthen client relationships. With these strategies, you can turn even the wildest escalation tornado into a gentle breeze of resolution.

"A diverse mix of voices leads to better discussions, decisions, and outcomes for everyone."

Sundar Pichai

10.0 Inclusion

Inclusion is like a party where everyone is invited; the more, the merrier. Instead of hors d'oeuvres and drinks, you get a diverse mix of people, perspectives, and ideas. Like at a party, you want everyone to feel welcome, comfortable, and valued. Inclusion isn't just about being polite; it's about creating a vibrant, dynamic atmosphere where everyone can contribute and have fun. It's not just about meeting diversity quotas or ticking boxes, but creating a workplace culture where everyone feels valued and can contribute their best work.

Better decision-making
Diverse and inclusive teams bring broader perspectives and experiences, leading to improved decision-making and more creative solutions. A team open to different viewpoints and ideas is more likely to develop innovative solutions and approaches.

Improved team morale

Team morale improves when everyone feels included and valued, increasing job satisfaction, engagement, and productivity. People are more likely to go above and beyond when they feel their contributions are valued and respected.

Increased innovation

When teams are inclusive, they are more likely to be innovative. Innovation is about creating new and better ways of doing things. A diverse and inclusive team can challenge assumptions, break down barriers, and find new approaches others may have overlooked.

Better client relationships

Inclusion can also improve client relationships. Clients are more likely to feel valued and respected when they see a diverse team working on their projects, leading to better communication, greater trust, and stronger partnerships.

Attracting and retaining top talent

Inclusion is also vital for attracting and retaining top talent. People want to work for companies that value diversity and inclusivity. When people feel included, they are more likely to stay with the company and recommend it to others.

Inclusion plays a critical role in achieving success. It leads to more informed decision-making, boosts team morale, sparks innovation, strengthens client relationships, and attracts top talent. Organisations that prioritise inclusion will undoubtedly reap the benefits of having a diverse and engaged workforce, ultimately paving the way for tremendous success. Fundamentally, prioritising inclusion is the right thing to do and a smart business strategy.

10.1 Unconscious bias

Unconscious bias refers to our subconscious attitudes or stereotypes that impact our decision-making and judgements towards certain groups of people. It can be based on various factors such as race, gender, age, ethnicity, religion, or other characteristics. It's like a pesky mosquito that won't leave you alone, no matter how often you swat at it. It keeps buzzing in your ear, distracting you from being objective. Similarly, unconscious bias can interfere with our ability to be fair and inclusive. By recognising our biases and taking steps to address them, we can swat that mosquito away and create a more inclusive environment where everyone can enjoy their picnic in peace with new friends from diverse backgrounds.

Reflect on your biases

It's essential to take a moment to reflect on your biases and understand where they come from. For example, if you realise that you hold biases against people of a particular gender, you can ask yourself why you have these biases. Do they stem from societal norms, past experiences, or personal beliefs? By understanding the root of your biases, you can begin to challenge them.

Meet new people

Interacting with people who are different from you can help you break down your biases. It may include attending cultural events, joining groups or clubs focusing on diversity, or striking up conversations with people different from you. The more exposure you have to other people and perspectives, the more likely you are to develop a greater sense of empathy and understanding.

Be mindful of your language

We must be mindful of our language and how it can perpetuate harmful stereotypes and biases. One example is using derogatory terms or slurs that reinforce sexist, racist, or discriminatory stereotypes. Such language can be hurtful and dehumanising, contributing to a culture of discrimination and prejudice.

Instead, we should strive to use inclusive and respectful language that does not marginalise or demean any group of people. By being conscious of our language, we can demonstrate our commitment to promoting equality and respect for all individuals.

Avoid microaggressions

Microaggressions are subtle, often unintentional actions or comments that can harm or offend marginalised individuals. These actions or words may seem harmless, but they can make people feel belittled, invalidated, or excluded. An example could be asking a person where they're "really" from, even if they were born and raised in the same country as you, making them feel like they are seen as an outsider or not entirely accepted in their own country.

Seek feedback

Sometimes, we may not even be aware of our biases. Seeking feedback from others can be a valuable way to gain insight. For example, ask a friend or colleague to provide feedback on how you interact with people who are different from you, helping you identify areas where you may need to work on your biases.

Unconscious bias is a pervasive issue that can negatively affect individuals and organisations. Identifying and overcoming unconscious bias requires self-awareness, empathy, education, and a commitment to change. We can overcome unconscious bias and create a more just and equitable society by challenging our assumptions, increasing our exposure to diverse perspectives, engaging in active listening, and fostering an inclusive culture.

10.2 Discrimination

Discrimination has no place in our society. It is an ugly and divisive force that causes harm and suffering to countless individuals and communities. While we may all have biases and prejudices, it is vital to actively combat discrimination and work towards a more inclusive and equitable world. Discrimination based on race, gender, sexuality, religion, or other characteristics can lead to significant social and economic inequalities. It also harms mental health, well-being, and overall quality of life. By actively opposing discrimination, we can create a more inclusive and welcoming society that values diversity and respects the rights and dignity of all people. Our collective responsibility is to stand against discrimination and work towards building a better world for everyone.

Educate yourself

One of the most critical steps in combating discrimination is to educate yourself about its various forms, which may include seeking out diverse perspectives and experiences, reading books, articles, and essays that address these issues, and listening to the experiences of marginalised individuals. For example, attending workshops, webinars, and training programmes on topics such as unconscious bias, microaggressions, and allyship can provide valuable insights and tools for challenging discrimination and bias.

Acknowledge your privilege

Privilege refers to the advantages and benefits that certain individuals or groups have, often based on factors such as race, gender, or socioeconomic status. One example of privilege is recognising the advantages of being born into a wealthy family. A person who grew up in a wealthy household may have had access to better education, healthcare, and opportunities for personal and professional development than someone from a lower socioeconomic background. By acknowledging this privilege, individuals can be more aware of the disparities and challenges faced by those who do not have the same advantages and work towards creating a more equitable society.

Speak up

If you witness discrimination in any form, speaking up and challenging it is essential. It can be as simple as calling out inappropriate language or as complex as engaging in difficult conversations with colleagues, friends, or family members who hold discriminatory beliefs. For example, if you hear someone making a racist joke or using derogatory language towards a particular group, you can intervene and explain why it is harmful and hurtful.

Be an ally

Being an ally means supporting marginalised communities in tangible ways. It may involve attending protests or rallies, donating to organisations that fight for social justice, or using your platform to amplify marginalised voices. For example, you can use your platform to highlight the experiences and perspectives of marginalised communities.

Hold yourself accountable

We all have biases, whether conscious or unconscious. It's important to recognise and challenge our preconceptions to ensure that we are not perpetuating discrimination. For example, suppose you notice that you prefer hiring people who share your background or experiences. In that case, you can actively seek candidates with diverse perspectives and experiences.

Discrimination is a destructive and pervasive force that has no place in our society. It is up to every one of us to actively combat discrimination and work towards a more inclusive and equitable world. It means educating ourselves on the various forms of discrimination, being mindful of our language, acknowledging our privilege, speaking up when we witness discrimination, being an ally to marginalised communities, and holding ourselves accountable for our biases. By taking these steps, we can create a society that values diversity and respects the rights and dignity of all people.

"Alone we can do so little; together we can do so much."

Helen Keller

11.0 Leadership

Regardless of your position within an organisation, it's never too early to develop the fundamental characteristics and practices essential for leadership. Effective leaders are like magicians in the workplace, conjuring up innovative solutions to complex problems. They have the charisma of a rockstar, the tenacity of a pit bull, and the ability to multitask like a mom on a mission. They must be skilled at navigating the complex world of office politics, motivating their team to reach new heights, maintaining their mental health, and persistently seeking opportunities for growth and development.

Lead by example

Leading by example is one of the most important ways to be an effective leader. It means demonstrating the behaviours and qualities that you expect from your team members. For example, if you want your team members to arrive on time, be punctual. If you want your team members to work hard and be dedicated, show them your commitment by working alongside them.

Communicate effectively

Ensure clear and concise communication while actively listening to your team members and offering constructive feedback. When giving feedback to a team member, be specific about your expectations, acknowledge their strengths, and identify areas for improvement. Be mindful of different communication styles and create a safe environment for quiet or introverted individuals.

Build a positive culture

Creating a positive work environment is essential for building a successful team and involves fostering an atmosphere of respect, trust, and collaboration. For example, you can encourage team members to share their ideas and opinions, recognise their accomplishments, and provide opportunities for them to learn and grow.

Be inclusive

Not everyone you'll work with will have the same background, working style, or experience. It's important to celebrate diversity and identify opportunities for team members to thrive by capitalising on their strengths. As the saying goes, "Everybody is a genius. But if you judge a fish by its ability to climb a tree, it will live its whole life believing that it is stupid."

Make sound decisions

As a leader, you will face many decisions that will impact your team and organisation. Making sound decisions requires being informed, analysing data, considering multiple perspectives, and weighing the pros and cons of each option. For example, if you are considering a new project, you should gather input from your team members, assess the feasibility, and evaluate the potential risks and benefits.

Empower and delegate

Effective leaders understand the importance of empowering and delegating tasks to their team members. They entrust team members with the authority and responsibility to make decisions and carry out tasks. For instance, if a team member has a particular skill set, a good leader would allow them to work on a project that utilises those skills, offering them trust and autonomy.

Continuously improve

Being an effective leader is an ongoing process that requires continuous improvement and may include seeking feedback from your team members, reflecting on your performance, and identifying areas for growth and development. For example, you can ask your team members for feedback on your leadership style, attend training programmes, and read books and articles on leadership.

Effective leadership is essential for the success of any organisation, and developing the fundamental characteristics and practices early on can pave the way for becoming a great consultant. Leading by example, communicating effectively, building a positive work environment, making sound decisions, empowering and delegating tasks, and continuous self-improvement are all key aspects of effective leadership. By following these practices, consultants can create a motivated and engaged team that can tackle complex challenges and achieve great results.

11.1 Jerks

Treating your colleagues, clients, and partners respectfully and professionally is essential in consulting, as in any other industry. Unfortunately, some people in the consulting world behave like jerks or assholes, making life difficult for everyone around them. It's like they have a sixth sense for detecting when you're having a good day and then swoop in to ruin it with their negative energy. These individuals tend to exhibit aggressive, selfish, and disrespectful behaviour towards others, creating a toxic work environment. They often belittle, criticise, and demean their coworkers, leading to low morale, decreased productivity, and high turnover rates. Frustratingly, they may be more interested in advancing their own careers and agendas than the team's or organisation's objectives, leading to a lack of cooperation, communication, and trust, which can ultimately hinder the success of the entire team or organisation. Therefore, leaders and managers must tackle negative behaviour and actively promote a culture characterised by respect, collaboration, and positivity.

Be respectful
It may seem like a no-brainer, but it's worth repeating: treat everyone with respect, regardless of their position or status, including your colleagues, clients, and partners. Don't belittle or talk down to anyone, and avoid using derogatory or offensive language.

Be collaborative
Consulting is a team sport; success often depends on working together effectively. Be willing to collaborate, share credit and recognition, and help others succeed. Don't try to hog the spotlight or take credit for others' work.

Be accountable
When things go wrong (and they often do in consulting), be willing to take responsibility for your actions and decisions. Don't blame others or make excuses; work to find solutions to problems rather than pointing fingers.

Be ethical

Integrity is a core value in consulting, and it's essential to always act with honesty and ethics. Avoid conflicts of interest, follow ethical guidelines and best practices, and be transparent in your dealings with others.

Be humble

Finally, it's crucial to maintain a sense of humility and perspective. Remember that you're not the most brilliant or important person in the room, and be open to learning from others. Avoid arrogance or overconfidence, and treat others as equals.

It is vital to exemplify qualities such as respect, collaboration, accountability, ethical behaviour, and humility to foster positive relationships and a thriving culture. Remember the adage, "Be the change you wish to see in the world." However, when confronted with the challenge of working with difficult individuals, it becomes necessary to assess your options. If the person causing difficulty is a junior team member, you could address the issue directly or involve their manager to intervene. On the other hand, if they hold a senior position, the situation becomes more complex. You may approach them directly to express your concerns or consider maintaining a healthy distance as they may resist change.

11.2 Brand

Establishing a personal brand is like creating a celebrity persona but for the corporate world. You must be the Taylor Swift of consulting or the Beyoncé of accounting. Instead of flamboyant outfits or immaculate choreography, you have to find other ways to showcase your expertise and value proposition in a way that makes people notice. It's like being a walking billboard for your awesomeness without the tacky neon lights and terrible puns.

Define your area of expertise

Consulting covers a broad range of industries and specialisations, so defining your area of expertise is crucial. Identify the sectors and types of consulting you specialise in, and focus on building your brand around that expertise. For example, a consultant specialising in healthcare could define their expertise as healthcare strategy and operations consulting. This focus allows them to tailor their communication and marketing efforts to healthcare organisations. It helps position them as an expert in their field.

Develop a strong value proposition

A strong value proposition is critical for establishing a personal brand in the consulting industry. Identify the unique value that you bring to the table and communicate it effectively to potential clients or employers. For example, a consultant specialising in sustainability could develop a value proposition around their ability to help companies reduce their environmental impact and save money through sustainable practices.

Leverage your network

Networking is critical for establishing a personal brand in the consulting industry. Leverage your network to build relationships with potential clients or employers and position yourself as a valuable asset in the industry. For instance, a consultant specialising in digital transformation could attend industry events, connect with other professionals on LinkedIn, and reach out to mentors or colleagues for advice and support.

Showcase your expertise
Consulting is all about expertise, so effectively showcasing your skills and knowledge is essential. Develop a robust online presence using social media platforms like LinkedIn or Twitter to share your insights and opinions on industry trends and issues. For example, a consultant specialising in organisational change could add posts that provide helpful tips and insights to organisations undergoing change management processes.

Stay up-to-date
Continuously invest in your professional development and education to stay relevant and competitive. For example, a consultant specialising in emerging technologies could attend conferences or workshops to keep up-to-date with the latest technological advancements and how they can be applied in their industry.

Be authentic
Finally, it's essential to be authentic when establishing a personal brand. Don't try to be someone you're not or over-hype your achievements. Instead, focus on communicating your unique skills and experiences in an honest and genuine way.

Establishing a personal brand in the consulting industry requires a combination of expertise, networking, and effective communication. By defining your area of expertise, developing a solid value proposition, leveraging your network, showcasing your expertise, and staying up-to-date with industry trends, you can establish a unique personal brand that positions you as a valuable asset and thought leader.

11.3 Mentorship

Having a mentor is like having a wise old wizard in your corner. Instead of casting spells, they cast pearls of wisdom and guidance. A mentor can be a valuable asset to anyone seeking personal or professional growth. Mentors are experienced professionals, typically in a similar industry or career path, who can provide guidance, support, and encouragement. They can offer valuable insights and knowledge, help identify opportunities and challenges, and provide feedback on performance.

Insights and knowledge

Mentors are often highly experienced professionals in your industry or field, several years ahead of you in their careers. They can offer guidance on specific skills and knowledge areas, provide feedback on performance, and help identify areas for improvement. Mentors can also offer insight into the industry, providing valuable information about trends, best practices, and opportunities.

Support and encouragement

Mentors can offer emotional and professional support, helping mentees navigate difficult situations and overcome challenges. Mentors can encourage and help build confidence, which is essential for success in any industry. They can also provide an objective perspective on situations, assisting mentees to gain clarity and make informed decisions.

Personal and career development

Mentors can help mentees identify their strengths and weaknesses, set goals, and develop action plans to achieve those goals. They can also guide career paths and help mentees identify new opportunities and challenges. Mentors can help mentees develop new skills, build relationships, and expand their professional networks.

Embracing a mentor's guidance can bring numerous advantages for individuals aspiring to enhance their development. Mentors possess a wealth of valuable insights and knowledge, offering support, encouragement, and the ability to recognise fresh opportunities. They play a pivotal role in helping individuals acquire new skills, advance their careers, and achieve their goals, significantly impacting personal and professional success. Therefore, if you have yet to find a mentor, actively seek one out, and remember to pay it forward by mentoring others when the opportunity arises.

11.4 Personal development

Personal development is the key to success unless your definition of success is to be a couch potato with a bag of chips permanently attached to your hand. In that case, personal development is probably not for you. It's like cleaning out your closet, but instead of getting rid of old clothes, you're getting rid of old habits, and we all have some bad habits. You may be a chronic procrastinator, or you may have a tendency to talk too much about your pet ferret. Personal development is the continuous process of enhancing oneself through activities that help to improve skills, knowledge, and overall well-being. It is an ongoing journey that requires dedication, commitment, and effort.

Set clear and specific goals

Setting specific, measurable, achievable, relevant, and time-bound (SMART) goals is essential for personal development. For instance, if you want to improve your public speaking skills, you could set a SMART goal of delivering a speech in front of a large audience within six months.

Take small steps

Personal development is a gradual process that requires patience and persistence. You need to break down your goals into small, manageable steps and celebrate your achievements along the way. For example, if you want to write a book, you can start by writing a page every day.

Seek feedback

Feedback helps you understand your strengths and weaknesses and identify areas for improvement. It's essential to seek input from people who are honest and constructive. You can ask for feedback from mentors, coaches, or colleagues.

Learn from failure

Failure is a natural part of personal development. It's crucial to learn from your mistakes and use them as opportunities for growth. Failure teaches you resilience, perseverance, and problem-solving skills.

Practice self-care

Personal development involves caring for your physical, emotional, and mental well-being. Self-care activities include exercising, eating well, getting enough sleep, practising mindfulness, and doing things that make you happy.

Learn continuously

Continuous learning is essential for personal development and includes attending courses, reading books, or listening to podcasts. For example, if you want to improve your leadership skills, read books on leadership, attend leadership seminars, or listen to podcasts featuring successful leaders.

Surround yourself with positive people

Your environment plays a significant role in your personal development. Surrounding yourself with positive and supportive people can motivate and inspire you to reach your goals. Avoid negative people who drain your energy and bring you down.

Personal development is an essential aspect of achieving success and happiness. By implementing these best practices, you can enhance your skills, knowledge, and overall well-being. Remember, personal growth is a journey, not a destination. Enjoy the process, and celebrate your achievements along the way.

11.5 Adaptability

Consulting is fast-paced and dynamic, and adapting quickly to new situations is critical for success. It's like being a chameleon; you must change your colours to match the environment. One day, you're a finance guru, and the next day, you're an IT wizard. The day after that, you're a marketing genius. Adaptable consultants are able to pivot quickly, adjust to new client needs, and find innovative solutions to complex problems.

Embrace change

Be open to new ideas and ways of doing things. Be willing to adapt your approach, including working with new technologies or methodologies, collaborating with different team members, or taking on new projects in unfamiliar industries. For example, if you're a consultant specialising in marketing, you might be asked to take on a project in the healthcare industry. While this might be outside your comfort zone, being adaptable means being willing to learn and adapt your marketing strategies to fit the healthcare industry's unique needs.

Stay agile

Another important aspect of being adaptable in consulting is staying agile and flexible, meaning pivoting when circumstances change and adjusting your approach to meet new challenges. For example, if a client wants to adjust the project scope, you'll need to be able to re-prioritize your tasks, change resources, and work efficiently to meet the revised objective.

Leverage new technologies

Technology is rapidly changing the consulting landscape, and adaptable consultants embrace and use new technologies to their advantage. For instance, a consultant working on a project that involves data analysis may use advanced AI-enabled analytics tools to gain insights and make recommendations to the client.

Anticipate challenges

Anticipating challenges and proactively addressing them is a critical skill for adaptable consultants. For example, a consultant working on a tight deadline may anticipate potential roadblocks and develop contingency plans to ensure the project is completed on time.

Learn continuously

Adaptable consultants are committed to continuous learning and professional development. They stay current on industry trends, attend conferences and training sessions, and seek opportunities to expand their knowledge and skills. For instance, a consultant in the energy industry may attend a conference on emerging energy trends to stay informed and provide valuable insights to clients.

Adaptability in consulting is a valuable and necessary trait in today's rapidly changing business landscape. It requires embracing change, staying agile, leveraging new technologies, anticipating challenges, and committing to continuous learning. Adaptable consultants are like chameleons, seamlessly adjusting their expertise to fit the specific needs of each project and client. So, be ready to change your colours, embrace new challenges, and confidently navigate the ever-evolving consulting terrain.

11.6 Trust

Trust is like a plant; you have to nurture it to make it grow. It is the foundation of any successful relationship, whether personal or professional. Building trust is a delicate and challenging process, but you can create beautiful relationships that bloom with consistency and care. Building and maintaining trust is essential for developing strong relationships with clients and colleagues, which is a cornerstone of success in any professional setting.

Demonstrate reliability

One of the most important ways to build trust is to demonstrate reliability, including showing up on time for meetings, responding to emails promptly, and delivering work on time and to a high standard. At its most basic, it is doing what you say you'll do. Clients and colleagues must feel confident they can rely on you to meet their expectations and deliver what you promised.

Be transparent

Clients want to work with consultants who are honest and transparent in their communication. It's all about being upfront about potential issues or challenges that may arise. For example, suppose you encounter an unexpected problem during a project that may cause a delay. In that case, it's vital to be transparent with the client and communicate the issue as soon as possible.

Establish clear expectations

Ensure that your team and the client clearly understand what the project entails, what the deliverables will be, and what the timeline for delivery is. For example, at the start of a project, it's essential to have a kickoff meeting with the client to discuss the scope of work, project timelines, and any other important details. By establishing clear expectations upfront, you can build trust with the client by showing that you are organised, professional, and committed to delivering on your promises.

Demonstrate expertise

Clients want to work with consultants who deeply understand their industry, business, or problem. Colleagues want to work with team members with the skills and knowledge to contribute to the project's success. To demonstrate your expertise, stay current on industry trends and share your insights with your colleagues and clients.

Be consistent

While anyone can display praiseworthy qualities in the short run, the actual test is consistently exhibiting those traits throughout an engagement or career. Demonstrating a consistent approach to communication, delivery, attention to detail, quality, and problem-solving can help establish a strong trust foundation.

Show empathy

Empathy means putting yourself in the client's shoes and understanding their needs and concerns. By doing so, you can better tailor your approach to the client. For example, imagine you're working with a client who is stressed out due to a complex project. You can build trust with the client and demonstrate your commitment to their success by showing empathy and offering support.

Building and maintaining trust is a vital aspect of any successful relationship. Trust requires nurturing, consistency, and care to grow and flourish. Establishing trust requires reliability, transparency, consistency, empathy, demonstrating expertise, and setting clear expectations. By prioritising trust-building in your professional relationships, you can set yourself up for long-term success and build a strong reputation in your firm.

"The best way to predict the future is to invent it."

Alan Kay

12.0 Exponential acceleration

The exponential acceleration of technology and change is revolutionising the world in unprecedented ways. From artificial intelligence and robotics to nanotechnology and quantum computing, technological advancements are transforming industries and reshaping human experiences. As breakthroughs occur with astonishing frequency, the complexity and interconnectedness of these developments can overwhelm even the most knowledgeable experts. Of course, the most exciting (or terrifying) aspect of exponential acceleration is that it will only continue to escalate in magnitude, meaning we are living in exciting times where the pace of change is simultaneously the fastest it has ever been and the slowest it will ever be again.

Our brains are wired for linear thinking
Human brains evolved to help us navigate our physical environment, where linear thinking was useful for survival, which means we tend to think in a straight line and assume that the future will be a continuation of the past. However, in today's world, where change is happening exponentially, linear thinking can be a hindrance.

It can cause us to underestimate the pace of change and miss opportunities for innovation and growth. Therefore, it is essential to be aware of our cognitive biases and to actively work to develop our ability to think non-linearly and adapt to the changing landscape of business and technology.

The pace is increasing

With technological advancements and the emergence of new industries, change is happening faster than ever. Every day, a new breakthrough, innovation, or disruption reshapes how we live, work, and interact with one another. This acceleration of change has created new challenges for businesses, governments, and individuals alike as they struggle to keep up with the rapid pace of transformation. Adapting to this new reality requires a shift in mindset and a willingness to embrace change and uncertainty. Those who can successfully navigate the accelerated pace of change are better positioned to thrive in today's fast-moving world.

Predicting the future is complicated

Numerous factors can influence future events, and many of them are unpredictable. The butterfly effect of exponential acceleration means that even small changes in the initial conditions or variables can result in significant differences in the outcomes. New technologies, social trends, and geopolitical factors can emerge rapidly and disrupt existing models and expectations. In the face of these challenges, consultants and organisations need to be increasingly agile and skilled at identifying trend lines to prepare for potential risks and opportunities.

The exponential acceleration of technology presents us with a world of endless possibilities and immense challenges, requiring innovative approaches, agility, and adaptability. For businesses and governments, it means rethinking structures and processes, fostering a culture of innovation and continuous learning, promoting collaboration and partnerships, and actively monitoring trends and emerging technologies.

For consultants, it means embracing lifelong continuous learning, adopting a flexible and iterative problem-solving approach, building diverse networks, and leveraging new technologies. There has never been a more exciting time to be in consulting, where we will need to navigate the challenges and disruptions of exponential acceleration while unlocking new opportunities for growth and innovation.

12.1 Artificial Intelligence

Artificial intelligence (AI) is the simulation of human intelligence in machines programmed to think and learn like humans. It involves the development of computer systems and algorithms capable of performing tasks that typically require human intelligence, such as problem-solving, pattern recognition, language understanding, and decision-making. AI encompasses a wide range of techniques, including machine learning, natural language processing, computer vision, and robotics, enabling machines to analyse data, make predictions, and automate processes with varying levels of autonomy. For consultants, it will be like having a personal assistant who does all the grunt work while we take all the credit.

Enhanced data analysis
Consultants often analyse vast amounts of data to uncover valuable insights. AI can rapidly process and analyse diverse data sets, enabling consultants to extract meaningful patterns and trends more efficiently. For instance, AI-powered data analytics tools can identify correlations and anomalies within complex financial data, helping consultants detect potential risks or uncover hidden opportunities. By automating time-consuming data analysis tasks, AI allows consultants to focus on higher-value activities, such as interpreting results and providing strategic recommendations.

Intelligent knowledge management

Consultants thrive on knowledge, but staying current with the latest industry trends, case studies, and best practices can be challenging. AI-powered knowledge management systems can help consultants access relevant information quickly and accurately. For example, AI-powered tools can analyse vast document, report, and article repositories, providing consultants with timely and tailored insights for their specific projects. These technologies enable consultants to stay informed, enhance their expertise, and deliver more comprehensive and innovative solutions.

Automated processes

AI-driven automation can significantly enhance the efficiency of consulting operations. For repetitive and time-consuming tasks, such as data entry, report generation, or data cleaning, AI-powered tools can automate processes, reducing human error and freeing consultants' time for higher-value work. For example, Natural Language Processing (NLP) tools can automate extracting and categorising information from large volumes of unstructured data, facilitating faster and more accurate insights. This automation allows consultants to focus on critical analysis and client engagement, ultimately delivering better outcomes.

Advanced decision support

Consultants often face complex decision-making scenarios that require thorough analysis and careful evaluation of multiple variables. AI can assist consultants by simulating different scenarios, predicting outcomes, and offering recommendations based on historical data. For instance, in strategic planning, AI-powered tools can generate sophisticated simulations to assess the impact of various strategies on business performance, empowering consultants to make more informed decisions and develop robust strategies aligning with their client's objectives.

New opportunities

AI is poised to disrupt every aspect of our lives, including how consulting services are delivered and the types of consulting services organisations procure. Traditional consulting services will be augmented with powerful AI tools, effectively improving their delivery capabilities. Meanwhile, organisations will be under ever-increasing pressure to deliver value rapidly, prompting them to adopt AI, digital twins, IoT, AR/VR, and other emerging technologies. By embracing these technologies, consultants can enhance their abilities and deliver more value to their clients, creating new opportunities for growth and innovation.

Artificial intelligence holds immense potential to transform the consulting industry. By enabling enhanced data analysis, intelligent knowledge management, automated processes, and advanced decision support, AI empowers consultants to deliver more efficient and impactful solutions. AI also opens up new opportunities for consultants to embrace emerging technologies and stay ahead in a rapidly evolving business landscape. As AI continues to advance, consultants who adopt and leverage its capabilities will be well-positioned to navigate the complexities of the future, ultimately driving growth, innovation, and value for their clients.

12.2 Revolution

The AI revolution is here. It's not like the robot uprisings you've seen in the movies. There won't be a hero who saves the day with a well-placed electromagnetic pulse or a dramatic monologue about the value of human life. While we don't have to worry about rampaging robots (just yet), the revolution's impacts are already significant, far-reaching, and disruptive. Every industry and business, including consulting, will experience profound shifts. AI will reshape the very foundations of consulting, from strategy and operations to legal and HR, finance and marketing, sales and IT. It is crucial to take proactive measures to remain competitive and prepared for the inevitable disruptions in our world. The time has come to embrace the power of AI and adapt to this new era of consulting.

Embrace continuous learning

To embrace the AI revolution, consultants must commit to continual learning and upskilling. Understanding the fundamentals of AI and emerging technologies becomes essential. Consultants should stay abreast of the latest trends, technologies, and applications relevant to their industry domains, enabling them to identify new opportunities and make informed decisions when recommending solutions to clients. For example, consider a marketing consultant who specialises in digital advertising. With the rapid advancements in AI-powered advertising platforms, continuous learning allows the consultant to understand and leverage the latest algorithms and strategies to deliver optimal client results. By staying abreast of evolving technologies and trends, the consultant remains competitive and capable of providing cutting-edge solutions in an ever-changing digital landscape.

Identify potential use cases

Once consultants have a strong understanding of AI, they can start determining potential use cases for their clients and within their organisations, whereby they evaluate business processes and pinpoint areas where AI can be applied.

For instance, a consultant operating in the retail sector might identify prospects for leveraging AI to enhance the customer experience. These opportunities may range from employing AI-driven chatbots for customer service to utilising AI for personalised recommendations or optimising pricing and promotional strategies. By strategically integrating AI, consultants can unlock significant improvements and drive tangible value for their clients.

Build partnerships

Consultants can proactively prepare themselves for the AI revolution by fostering collaborations with AI companies or startups. By forming strategic partnerships, consultants can harness these companies' specialised expertise and cutting-edge technology to deliver enhanced value to their clients. For instance, a consultant operating in the financial services sector could establish a partnership with an AI startup specialising in fraud detection. This collaboration would empower the consultant to offer their clients a more robust and comprehensive fraud detection solution, leveraging the advanced capabilities of the AI startup. By embracing such partnerships, consultants can stay at the forefront of AI innovation and provide tailored solutions that address evolving client needs.

Stay focused on ethical considerations

As AI evolves, it is crucial to consider its ethical implications. AI algorithms have the potential to perpetuate biases or produce unintended outcomes, making it imperative to ensure the ethical development and deployment of AI systems. A prime example of this approach is Google, which has established ethical principles for AI. These principles encompass dedication to fairness, accountability, and transparency, reflecting the commitment to upholding ethical standards in AI utilisation. By adhering to such principles and continuously evaluating the ethical implications of AI, we can ensure the responsible and beneficial integration of AI technologies into our society.

The AI revolution should not be feared; instead, it presents an opportunity for consultants to embrace innovation and drive value. By actively learning about AI, identifying potential use cases, fostering partnerships, continuously developing AI skills, and focusing on ethical considerations, consultants can position themselves at the forefront of this transformative era. It is crucial to approach the revolution with an open mind, curiosity, and readiness to adapt to AI's exciting possibilities. Let us seize this opportunity to shape the future and unlock the immense potential of AI in delivering exceptional results for our clients.

"Luck is what happens when preparation meets opportunity."

Seneca

Conclusion

Congratulations! You made it to the end of this handbook. I hope that you've found it helpful, informative, and maybe even a little entertaining.

Throughout this book, we have explored the intricacies of the consulting industry and delved into the challenges, triumphs, and dynamic nature of this profession. However, amidst all the analysis, strategies, and methodologies, it is essential to remember that consulting is a human-centred profession at its core. It's more than just numbers, spreadsheets, and presentations. It's about people, including colleagues, clients, and communities impacted by our work.

Every project, recommendation, and decision ultimately revolves around the individuals involved. The essence of consulting lies in striving to understand all stakeholders' unique needs, goals, and aspirations. It requires active listening, empathy, and building trusted relationships. It is about immersing ourselves in their world, putting ourselves in their shoes, uncovering opportunities, and co-creating solutions that truly make a difference.

In addition to looking outward, we must also make time for self-reflection. In conjunction with the advice and feedback provided by our colleagues, families, and mentors, introspection offers invaluable insights into our strengths, weaknesses, and development areas. By nurturing a growth mindset, continuous personal development, and prioritising self-care, we can proactively shape our career trajectories and better support those around us. Always remember to stay humble and find ways to pay it forward.

Finally, as the pace of change only accelerates, we must constantly seek new knowledge, challenge our assumptions, and be open to unlearning and relearning. No single individual possesses all the answers or expertise needed to tackle complex challenges. By fostering a culture of collaboration and inclusion, we can leverage the collective intelligence and diverse perspectives of our colleagues, clients, and external partners. Collaborative approaches lead to better outcomes and foster a shared sense of ownership and commitment to driving meaningful change.

Your career in consulting or elsewhere will undoubtedly be a rollercoaster ride, filled with incredible highs and agonising lows. Throughout it all, take time to put things in perspective, celebrate your victories, use adversity as an opportunity to learn, and always try to maintain your sense of humour. It's going to be an exhilarating ride!

How (Not) to Fail at Consulting

Having turned the last page of the *Consulting Handbook*, you might be eager to delve deeper into the consulting world and learn from industry leaders to improve your career trajectory, relationships, teams, and organisations.

How (Not) to Fail at Consulting could be your next great read. It is a contemporary, practical guide to management consulting told through vignettes, stories, and personal accounts of people who have lived the consulting life and have the battle scars to prove it. The book offers an engaging, brutally honest, no-holds-barred glimpse into the world of consulting, where you'll find firsthand and research-based insights into personal and career development, leadership, strategy, communication, adversity, networking, human-centred design, diversity, mental health, and trends that will shape the consulting industry in the years to come.

Check it out on Amazon or learn more at www.hownottofailatconsulting.com.

The next chapter of your consulting journey awaits.

Jack Przemieniecki

An experienced consultant, entrepreneur, and advocate for human-centred design, Jack has spent over twenty years working with innovative start-ups, entrepreneurial agencies, and industry-leading consultancies. Having worked across four continents with some of the world's most recognisable brands, he has seen the good, the bad and the ugly sides of the consulting world. He continues to help organisations and start-ups identify innovative opportunities, mentors and supports others within numerous communities, and advocates for a more inclusive, diverse, and just society. When not writing or working, he can be found staying active, discovering new restaurants, enjoying a good movie, or continuing to explore the world.